Arduino Android Blueprints

GW00808629

Get the best out of Arduino by interfacing it with Android to create engaging interactive projects

Marco Schwartz

Stefan Buttigieg

[PACKT] PUBLISHING open source
community experience distilled

BIRMINGHAM - MUMBAI

Arduino Android Blueprints

First published: December 2014

Production reference: 1151214

Published by Packt Publishing Ltd.
Livery Place
35 Livery Street
Birmingham B3 2PB, UK.

ISBN 978-1-78439-038-9

www.packtpub.com

Credits

Authors
Marco Schwartz
Stefan Buttigieg

Reviewers
Simone Bianchi
Kyrre Havik Eriksen
Adam Laskowitz
Rufael Negash

Commissioning Editor
Nadeem N. Bagban

Acquisition Editor
Harsha Bharwani

Content Development Editor
Anand Singh

Technical Editor
Indrajit A. Das

Copy Editors
Janbal Dharmaraj
Vikrant Phadkay

Project Coordinator
Rashi Khivansara

Proofreaders
Martin Diver
Maria Gould
Samantha Lyon

Indexer
Hemangini Bari

Production Coordinator
Nitesh Thakur

Cover Work
Nitesh Thakur

About the Authors

Marco Schwartz is an electrical engineer, entrepreneur, and blogger. He has a Master's degree in Electrical Engineering and Computer Science from Supélec in France and a Master's degree in Micro Engineering from the EPFL in Switzerland.

He has more than 5 years of experience working in the domain of electrical engineering. His interests gravitate around electronics, home automation, the Arduino and Raspberry Pi platforms, open source hardware projects, and 3D printing.

He runs several websites around Arduino, including the Open Home Automation website, which is dedicated to building home automation systems using open source hardware.

He has written another book on home automation and Arduino, called *Home Automation with Arduino* and another book on how to build the Internet of Things projects with Arduino, called *Internet of Things with the Arduino Yún, Packt Publishing*.

Stefan Buttigieg is a medical doctor, mobile developer, and entrepreneur. He graduated as a Doctor of Medicine and Surgery at the University of Malta, and he is currently enrolled at the University of Sheffield where he is undertaking a Master's degree in Health Informatics.

He has more than 5 years of experience working in various technical positions in international and local student organizations, and has founded MD Geeks, an online community that brings health professionals, developers, and entrepreneurs together from around the world to share their passion for the intersection of healthcare and information technology.

His main interests are in mobile development, specifically, Android and iOS, open source healthcare projects, user interface design, mobile user experience, and project management.

I would like to thank Angelika Biernacka-Buttigieg, my wife, for her unconditional support and patience throughout the creation of this book.

My parents, Joseph Buttigieg and Anne Buttigieg, for their support for this book project.

Christopher Svanefalk for his amazing insight and patience with code reviews and support.

Don Coleman, for his invaluable help in *Chapter 8, Control an Arduino Board via NFC*. We recommend his expertise on near field communication technologies.

About the Reviewers

Simone Bianchi lives in Italy, where after a degree in electronic engineering, he started to work as a programmer developing web applications using technologies such as Java, JSP, JQuery, and Oracle. When time permits, he likes to explore other topics, contribute to the open source community developing free components for the Talend Platform (for example, the tDBFInput and tDBFOutput components), develop Android apps (SleepyTimer), or return to the subjects of his studies, delighting himself building small IoT projects using microcontrollers like the ones of the Arduino family.

I'd like to thank Pack Publishing for again giving me the opportunity to review their book after *Talend for Big Data*, and I hope you can find this book as inspiring as it has been for me reviewing it.

Kyrre Havik Eriksen is an independent and curious person, with a Master's degree in Informatics from the University of Oslo, Norway. He works full time as a Java developer, but in his spare time, he studies Android and game development with Löve and Libgdx. He has also taught Processing and Arduino while he studied.

Adam Laskowitz received his Master's degree in Architecture and Master's degree in Fine Arts from the University at Buffalo in 2012. Adam has designed and built a number of interactive installations, notably Diep International Art Festival in 2011, Dieppe, France; SIGGRAPH in 2012, Los Angeles, CA; and HERE Art Center in 2013, New York. Adam has worked as a designer, researcher, and prototyper at Intel Labs and Intel New Devices Group. In October 2014, he joined Target Technology Innovation Center as an experience design lead. He has been featured in a number of articles and productions, including a BBC interview discussing citizen science and air quality research.

Rufael Negash is an interaction designer and creative coder, based in Malmö, Sweden.

www.PacktPub.com

Support files, eBooks, discount offers, and more

For support files and downloads related to your book, please visit www.PacktPub.com.

Did you know that Packt offers eBook versions of every book published, with PDF and ePub files available? You can upgrade to the eBook version at www.PacktPub.com and as a print book customer, you are entitled to a discount on the eBook copy. Get in touch with us at service@packtpub.com for more details.

At www.PacktPub.com, you can also read a collection of free technical articles, sign up for a range of free newsletters and receive exclusive discounts and offers on Packt books and eBooks.

https://www2.packtpub.com/books/subscription/packtlib

Do you need instant solutions to your IT questions? PacktLib is Packt's online digital book library. Here, you can search, access, and read Packt's entire library of books.

Why subscribe?

- Fully searchable across every book published by Packt
- Copy and paste, print, and bookmark content
- On demand and accessible via a web browser

Free access for Packt account holders

If you have an account with Packt at www.PacktPub.com, you can use this to access PacktLib today and view 9 entirely free books. Simply use your login credentials for immediate access.

Table of Contents

Preface

When directly comparing Arduino and Android, one can see that they are two incredibly different platforms with different targets. Arduino is mostly focused on connecting physical everyday objects to embedded microcontrollers. On the other hand, Android intends to provide the necessary operating system and framework to operate countless smartphones around the world.

This reality also reflects the contrasting realities of the authors, who come from very different backgrounds and cultures; Stefan hails from the Island of Malta, and he brings with him a medical background and passion for the intersection of technology and medicine, whereas Marco originates from France and has an electrical engineering background.

The power of combining the efforts of Arduino and Android platforms bring about incredibly implemented practical projects that enhance daily life. Keeping this motivation in mind is what brought two authors from contrasting backgrounds together to work on this book. We believe in the intersection of technology and real life and visualize a future where technology will keep on forming an integral part of our day-to-day life.

What this book covers

Chapter 1, Setting Up Your Workspace, covers the necessary steps that you will have to take in order to build all the projects of the book. You will learn how to set up the Android development environment. We will also build our first Arduino project.

Chapter 2, Controlling an Arduino Board via Bluetooth, teaches us how to link Arduino and Android for the first time. We will build an Arduino system with a Bluetooth Low Energy module, and control a simple LED from an Android application.

Chapter 3, Bluetooth Weather Station, teaches us how to build our first useful application using Arduino and Android. We will build a weather measurement station, and visualize the measurements via an Android application, which we will build from scratch.

Chapter 4, Wi-Fi Smart Power Plug, teaches us how to build a DIY version of a popular device: a wireless power switch. We will use an Android application to communicate with the switch via Wi-Fi, control it, and measure the energy consumption of the connected device.

Chapter 5, Wi-Fi Remote Security Camera, introduces a powerful Arduino board, the Arduino Yún, to build a DIY wireless security camera. We will also build an Android application to monitor this camera remotely from an Android phone.

Chapter 6, Android Phone Sensor, explains how to turn things around, and use the sensors from our phone to control the Arduino board. Applying this, we will use the gyroscope of the phone to control the angle of a servomotor.

Chapter 7, Voice-activated Arduino, teaches us how to use the powerful Android speech API to control an Arduino board via Bluetooth.

Chapter 8, Control an Arduino Board via NFC, shows how to use the NFC chip present in many Android phones to activate a relay connected to an Arduino board.

Chapter 9, Bluetooth Low Energy Mobile Robot, uses everything we learned so far in the book to build a mobile robot based on the Arduino. The robot will be controlled via Wi-Fi from an Android application.

Chapter 10, Pulse Rate Sensor, is dedicated to a medical application that measures the heart rate. We will connect a heart rate sensor to Arduino and monitor the measurements via Bluetooth Low Energy.

What you need for this book

You will need two kind of software for this book: the software you will need for Arduino, and the software you will need for Android. For Arduino, here is what you will need in all chapters:

- Arduino IDE (Version 1.5.7 is recommended)

You will also need several Arduino libraries depending on the chapter, but the links to these libraries are given in the relevant chapters.

On the Android side, you will need the following:

- Android Studio
- Android 4.3 or higher on your Android phone

Who this book is for

Arduino Android Blueprints is aimed for anyone who is knowledgeable in either the Arduino or Android ecosystems and who would like to get started with building exciting applications using both platforms.

For example, this book is for you if you are already using the Arduino platform and you want to build mobile applications to control your projects remotely.

Conventions

In this book, you will find a number of styles of text that distinguish between different kinds of information. Here are some examples of these styles, and an explanation of their meaning.

Code words in text, database table names, folder names, filenames, file extensions, pathnames, dummy URLs, user input, and Twitter handles are shown as follows: "Your `Arduino` folder is where all the sketches are stored, and you can define this folder in the preferences of the Arduino IDE."

A block of code is set as follows:

```
android:textSize="200dp"
    android:gravity="center"
```

Any command-line input or output is written as follows:

```
/distance
```

New terms and **important words** are shown in bold. Words that you see on the screen, in menus or dialog boxes for example, appear in the text like this: "Depending on your device, this option might vary slightly, but as from Android 4.2 and higher, the **Developer options** screen is hidden by default."

[Warnings or important notes appear in a box like this.]

[Tips and tricks appear like this.]

Reader feedback

Feedback from our readers is always welcome. Let us know what you think about this book—what you liked or may have disliked. Reader feedback is important for us to develop titles that you really get the most out of.

To send us general feedback, simply send an e-mail to `feedback@packtpub.com`, and mention the book title via the subject of your message.

If there is a topic that you have expertise in and you are interested in either writing or contributing to a book, see our author guide on `www.packtpub.com/authors`.

Customer support

Now that you are the proud owner of a Packt book, we have a number of things to help you to get the most from your purchase.

Downloading the example code

You can download the example code files for all Packt books you have purchased from your account at `http://www.packtpub.com`. If you purchased this book elsewhere, you can visit `http://www.packtpub.com/support` and register to have the files e-mailed directly to you.

Downloading the color images of this book

We also provide you a PDF file that has color images of the screenshots/diagrams used in this book. The color images will help you better understand the changes in the output. You can download this file from: `http://www.packtpub.com/sites/default/files/downloads/03890S_ColorImages.pdf`.

Errata

Although we have taken every care to ensure the accuracy of our content, mistakes do happen. If you find a mistake in one of our books—maybe a mistake in the text or the code—we would be grateful if you could report this to us. By doing so, you can save other readers from frustration and help us improve subsequent versions of this book. If you find any errata, please report them by visiting `http://www.packtpub.com/submit-errata`, selecting your book, clicking on the **Errata Submission Form** link, and entering the details of your errata. Once your errata are verified, your submission will be accepted and the errata will be uploaded to our website or added to any list of existing errata under the Errata section of that title.

To view the previously submitted errata, go to `https://www.packtpub.com/books/content/support` and enter the name of the book in the search field. The required information will appear under the **Errata** section.

Piracy

Piracy of copyright material on the Internet is an ongoing problem across all media. At Packt, we take the protection of our copyright and licenses very seriously. If you come across any illegal copies of our works, in any form, on the Internet, please provide us with the location address or website name immediately so that we can pursue a remedy.

Please contact us at `copyright@packtpub.com` with a link to the suspected pirated material.

We appreciate your help in protecting our authors, and our ability to bring you valuable content.

Questions

If you have a problem with any aspect of this book, you can contact us at `questions@packtpub.com`, and we will do our best to address the problem.

1
Setting Up Your Workspace

The first chapter of this book will teach you the basics of the Arduino and Android development so that you can be sure you have the basics required for the more advanced tutorials you will find in the rest of this book.

On the Arduino side, we will build a very simple project with a relay module (which is basically a switch that can be controlled with Arduino) and a temperature and humidity sensor. We will also see the basics of the Arduino IDE and the basic commands of the aREST library, which is a framework to easily control Arduino boards. We will use this library in several chapters of this book to make it really easy to control the Arduino board from an Android device. In this first chapter, we will simply try out the commands of the aREST library by having the Arduino board connected to your computer via a USB.

From the Android development point of view, we will work together to set up a development environment and ensure that your computer and the Android device are ready for development purposes. We will start off with a simple Android app that displays the legendary text, **Hello World**.

Android Studio is an IntelliJ-based **Integrated Development Environment (IDE)** fully supported by the Android development team, which will provide you with the necessary tools and resources to make sure that you develop a functional and aesthetic Android app.

Android Studio is in beta but the software is updated on a frequent and regular basis by a dedicated team at Google, which makes it the natural choice to develop our Android projects.

Hardware and software requirements

The first thing you will need is an Arduino Uno board. We will use this board throughout this book to connect sensors, actuators, and wireless modules and make them interact with Android. Then, we will need a relay module. A relay is basically an electrical switch that we can command from Arduino, which can allow us to control devices such as lamps. This project uses a 5V relay module from Polulu, which properly integrates a relay on a board, along with all the required components to control the relay from Arduino. The following is the image of the relay module that was used in this chapter:

You will also need a DHT11 (or DHT22) sensor, along with a 4.7K resistor, for temperature and humidity measurements. A resistor is basically a device to limit the current flowing into an electrical device. Here, it is necessary to ensure the correct functioning of the DHT sensor.

Finally, you will need a small breadboard and jumper wires to make the different hardware connections.

The following is the list of all hardware parts you will need for this project, along with links to find these parts on the Web:

- The Arduino Uno board (`http://www.adafruit.com/product/50`)
- The 5V relay module (`http://www.pololu.com/product/2480`)
- The DHT11 sensor and 4.7K Ohm resistor (`https://www.adafruit.com/product/386`)
- The breadboard (`https://www.adafruit.com/product/64`)
- Jumper wires (`https://www.adafruit.com/product/758`)

On the software side, you will need the Arduino IDE that we will also use in the rest of this book. You can get it at `http://arduino.cc/en/Main/Software`.

The installation process of the IDE is very simple; you simply have to open the file and follow the onscreen instructions.

You will need the library for the DHT11 sensor, which can be found at `https://github.com/adafruit/DHT-sensor-library`.

You will also need the aREST library found at `https://github.com/marcoschwartz/aREST`.

To install a given library, simply extract the folder in your `Arduino/libraries` folder (or create this folder if it doesn't exist yet). Your `Arduino` folder is where all the sketches are stored, and you can define this folder in the preferences of the Arduino IDE.

Preparing for Android development requires that we get ready to design and develop the app, and the following checklist will guide you with having the basics ready for any project:

- Java Developer Kit Version 6 (or higher)
- Android Studio
- Android Software Development Kit
- Android Device with Bluetooth SMART technology

We will also work together to make sure that you have everything properly set up.

Installing Java Developer Kit

Android Studio will not work without **Java Developer Kit** (**JDK**); therefore, it's necessary to know what Java version you have installed (in this particular case, the Java Runtime Environment will not be enough).

Checking the JDK version

It is mandatory that you check the version of your JDK for compatibility purposes.

Mac

Open Terminal and type the following command:

```
java -version
```

This is what will be shown on the screen:

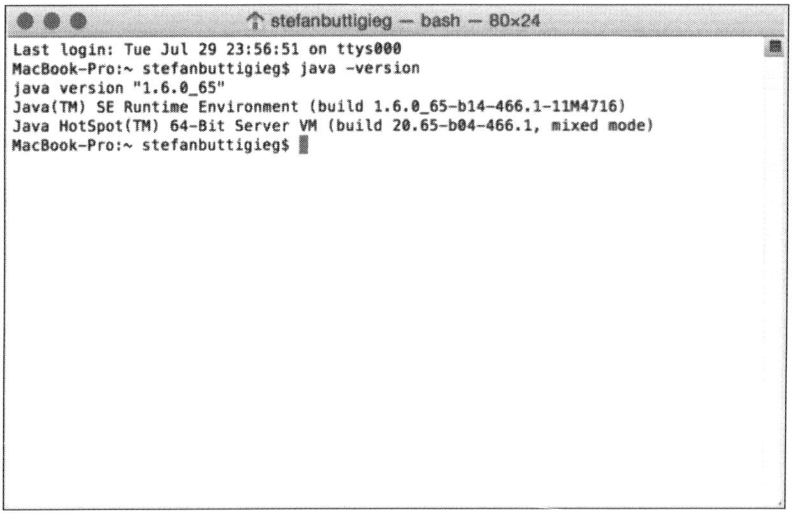

Windows

Open Command Prompt and type the following command:

```
java -version
```

This is what will be shown on the screen:

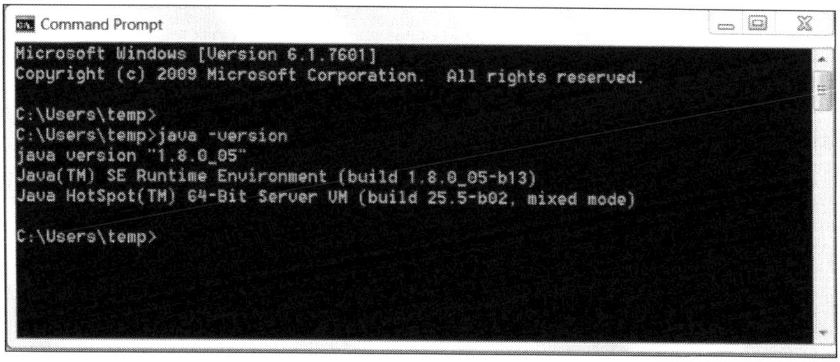

Installing Java

If you do not have Java installed, or if your version is below 6.0, install the Java JDK by clicking on the following customized and shortened link and choosing the version that applies for you:

http://j.mp/javadevkit-download

The following window will open:

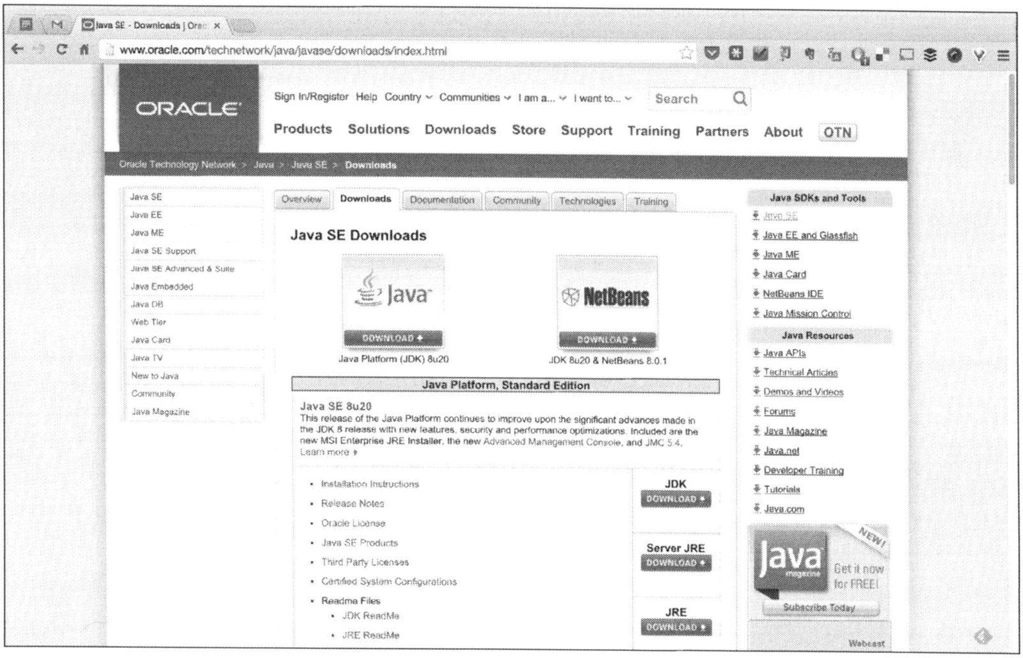

The main recommendation for these projects is that you install a version of JDK 6.0 or higher.

Select the JDK for your operating system. On an Intel-based Mac, you can follow this useful table to see whether your Mac is 32-bit or 64-bit:

Processor Name	32- or 64-bit processor
Intel Core Solo	32 bit
Intel Core Duo	32 bit
Intel Core 2 Duo	64 bit
Intel Quad-Core Xeon	64 bit
Dual-Core Intel Xeon	64 bit
Quad-Core Intel Xeon	64 bit
Core i3	64 bit
Core i5	64 bit
Core i7	64 bit

You can check for **Processor Name** by clicking on the Apple logo in the top-left corner of your screen followed by **About my Mac**.

In the case of Windows, to see whether your computer is running a 32-bit or 64-bit version of Windows, you need to do the following:

1. Click on the Start button.
2. Right-click on **My Computer**, and then click on **Properties**. If **x64 edition** is listed under system, your processor is capable of running 64-bit-enabled applications.

Installing Android Studio

Let's see how we install Android Studio on Mac and Windows:

1. Go to the Android Developers site at `http://developer.android.com`. The following screen will appear:

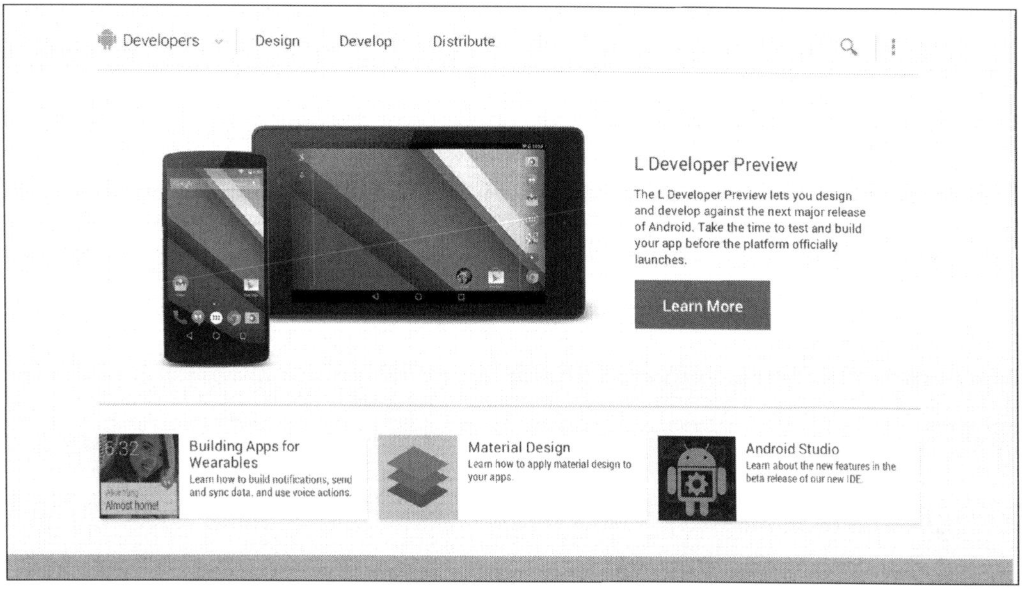

2. Click on **Android Studio**; you will be directed to the landing page where your operating system version will be detected automatically, as shown in the following screenshot:

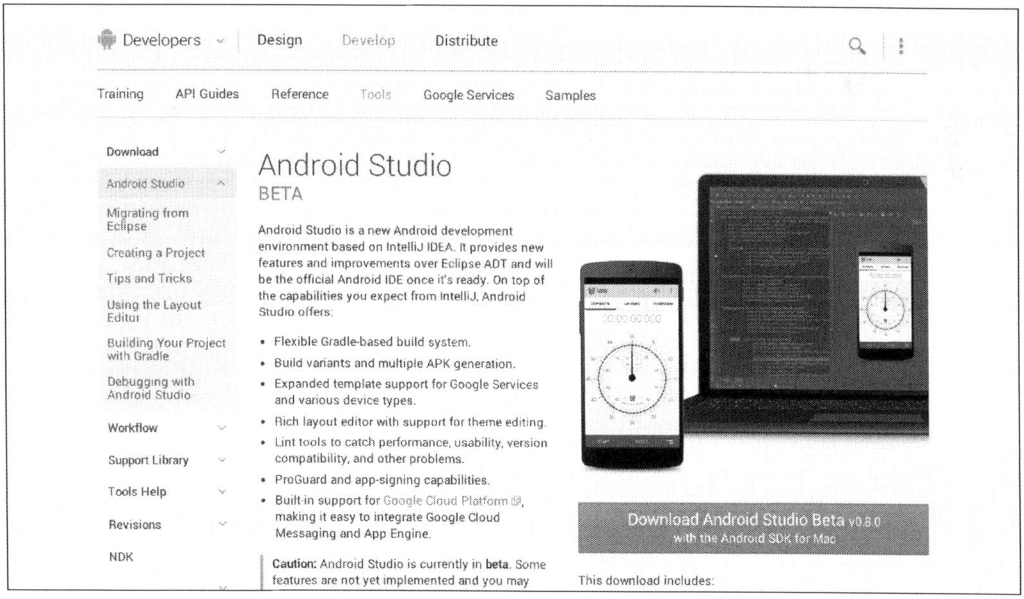

3. Accept the **Terms and Conditions** of the software use agreement:

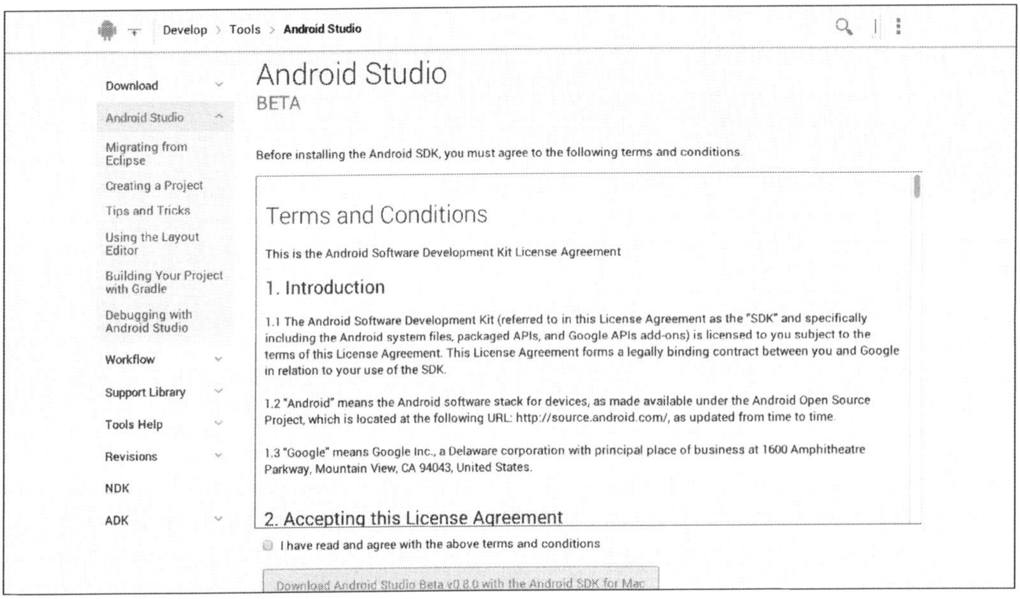

Mac

Double-click on the downloaded file, follow the prompts, and then drag the Android Studio icon into your `Applications` folder:

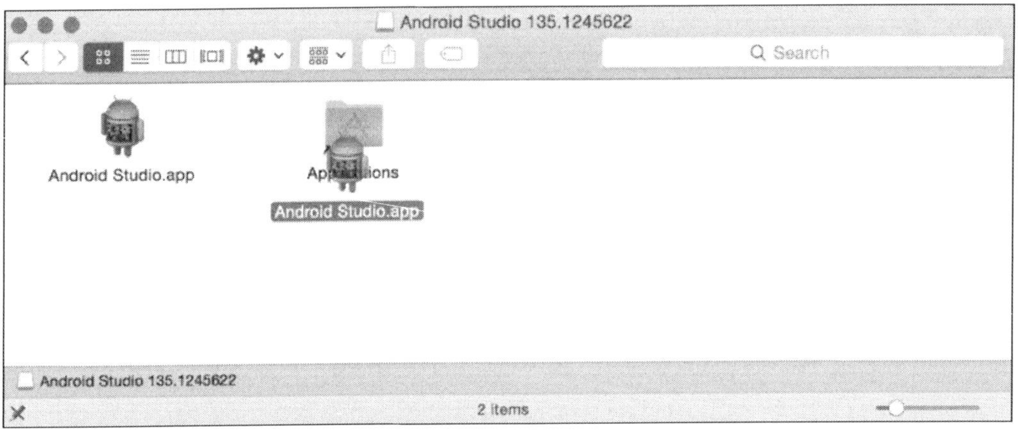

Windows

Open the downloaded file, and then go through the following **Android Studio Setup Wizard** window to complete the installation process:

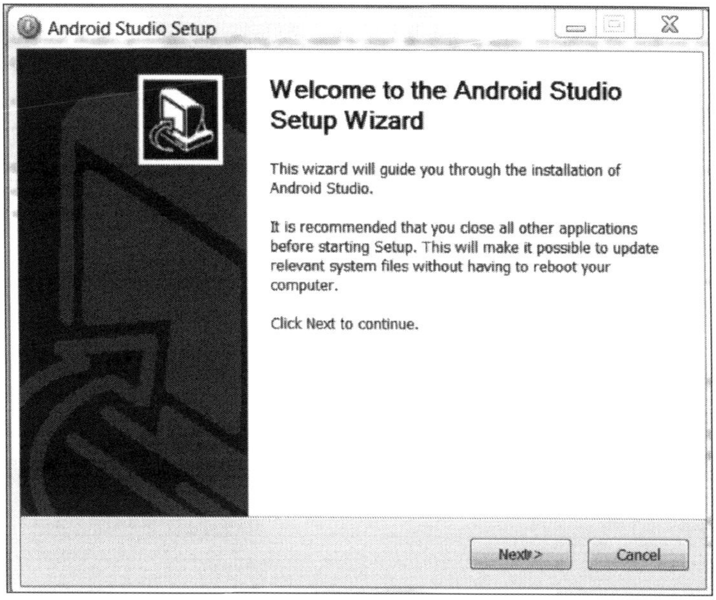

Setting up the Android Software Development Kit

The process of setting up the Android **Software Development Kit** (**SDK**) has improved vastly with the introduction of Android Studio, as the latest SDKs come preinstalled with the Android Studio install package. In order to develop the projects detailed in the following chapters, it would be very helpful to understand how you can install (or even uninstall) SDKs within Android Studio.

There are a number of ways to access the **SDK Manager**. The most straightforward way is through the following Android Studio main toolbar:

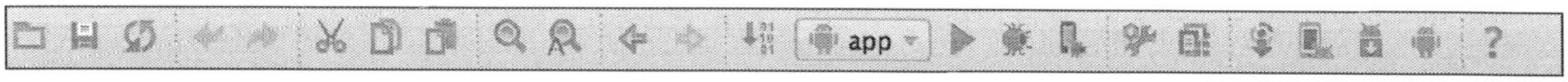

Another option would be via the **Launch** menu where you will be faced with the following options:

In order to access the SDK Manager, you will need to click on **Configure**, where the following screen will appear, and then click on **SDK Manager**:

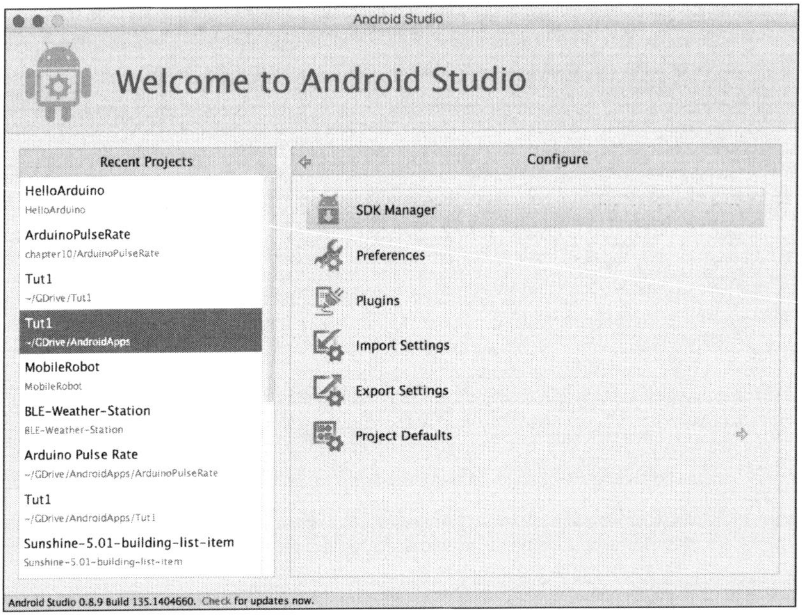

The previous screenshot shows us what the SDK Manager looks like. If you need to install any packages, you need to check the mark of that particular package, click on **Install packages**, and then finally accept the licenses, as shown in the following screenshot:

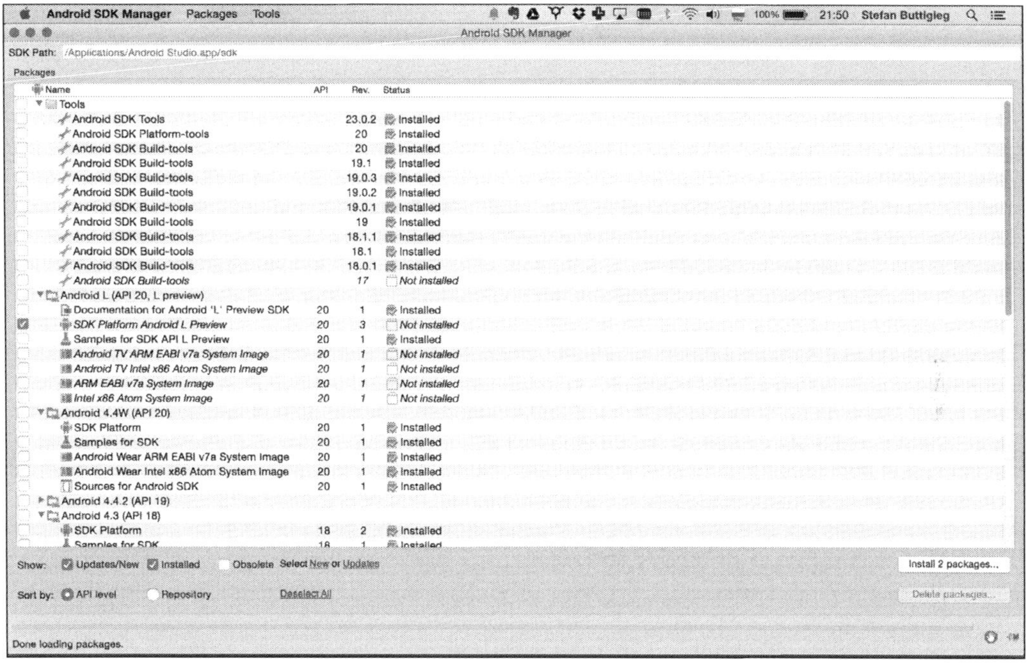

Setting up your physical Android device for development

The following are the three main steps that need to be executed in order to enable your Android device for development:

1. Enable **Developer options** on your specific Android device.
2. Enable **USB debugging**.
3. Entrust the computer with an installed IDE via secure USB debugging (devices with Android 4.4.2).

Enabling Developer options

Depending on your device, this option might vary slightly, but from Android 4.2 and higher, the **Developer options** screen is hidden by default.

To make it available, go to **Settings** | **About phone** and tap on **Build number** seven times. You will find **Developer options** enabled by returning to the previous screen.

Enabling USB debugging

USB debugging enables the IDE to communicate with the device via the USB port. This can be activated after enabling **Developer options** and is done by checking the **USB debugging** option by navigating to **Settings** | **Developer options** | **Debugging** | **USB debugging**.

Entrusting the computer with the installed IDE using secure USB debugging (devices with Android 4.4.2)

You have to accept the RSA key on your phone or tablet before anything can flow between the device via **Android Debug Bridge** (**ADB**). This is done by connecting the device to the computer via a USB, which triggers a notification entitled **Enable USB Debugging**.

Check **Always allow from this Computer** followed by clicking on **OK**.

Hardware configuration

For the first project of this book, there are only a few hardware connections to make. We simply need to connect the relay module and the DHT11 sensor to the Arduino board.

The following image summarizes the hardware connections for this chapter (with the DHT sensor on the left of the breadboard, and the relay module on the right):

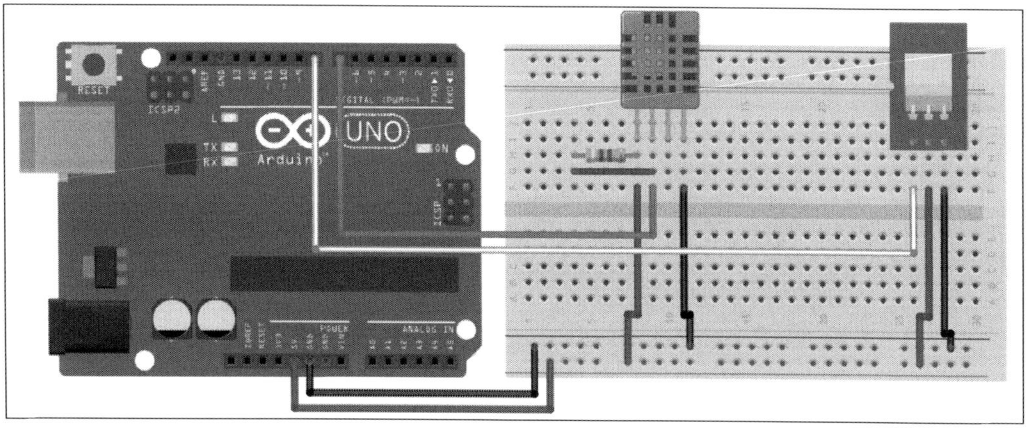

The first thing you need to do is to connect the power from the Arduino board to the power rails on the side of the breadboard. Connect the Arduino 5V pin to the red power rail on the breadboard, and the Arduino GND pin to the blue power rail on the breadboard.

For the DHT11 sensor, you first need to have a look at the pins configuration of the sensor by visiting `http://www.rlocman.ru/i/Image/2012/09/06/DHT11_Pins.jpg`.

You need to first connect the power supply; the VCC pin goes to the red power rail on the breadboard, and the GND pin goes to the blue power rail. You also need to connect the DATA pin to pin number 7 of the Arduino board. Finally, place the 4.7K Ohm resistor between the VCC and the DATA pin of the sensor.

For the relay module, you have three pins to connect: VCC, GND, and SIG. Connect the VCC pin to the red power rail on the breadboard, GND to the blue power rail, and finally, connect the SIG pin to Arduino pin 8.

The following is an image of the completely assembled project:

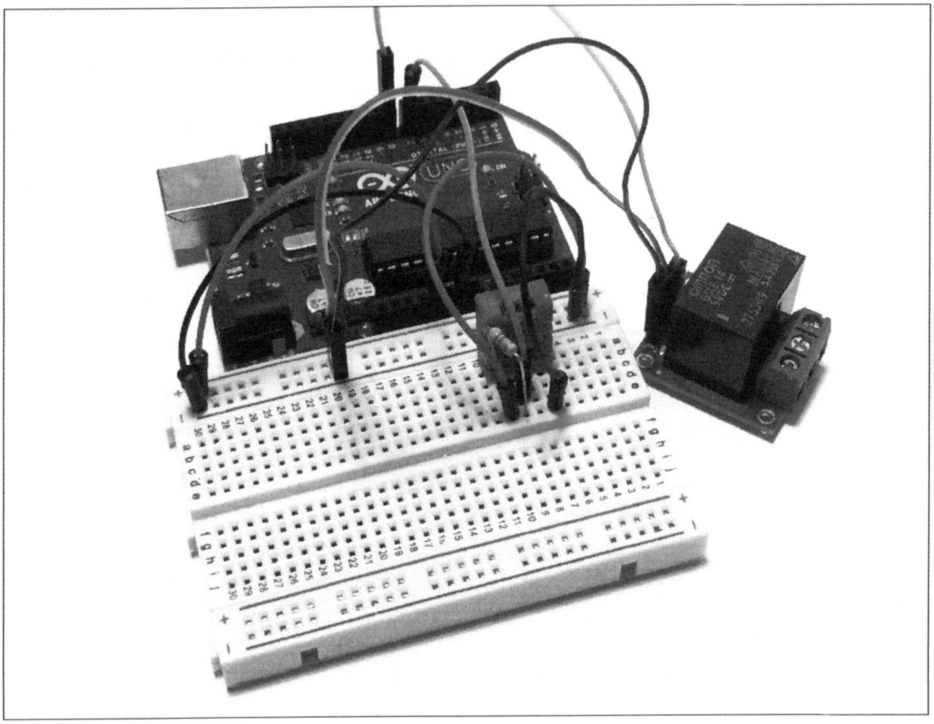

Learning to use the aREST library

Now that our hardware is assembled, we are going to see the basics of the Arduino environment, and how to use the aREST library that we are going to use in several chapters of this book to control Arduino from an Android phone.

The aREST library will allow us to simply control the Arduino board externally using the same commands, whether it is using an USB cable, Bluetooth, or Wi-Fi. Without this library, we will have to rewrite the same code several times for all the chapters of the book. To find a complete documentation on the aREST library, you can visit `https://github.com/marcoschwartz/aREST`.

The main window of the Arduino IDE is where you enter the code to program the Arduino board.

Arduino code files are usually called **sketches**. The following screenshot is of the Arduino IDE with the code of this chapter already loaded:

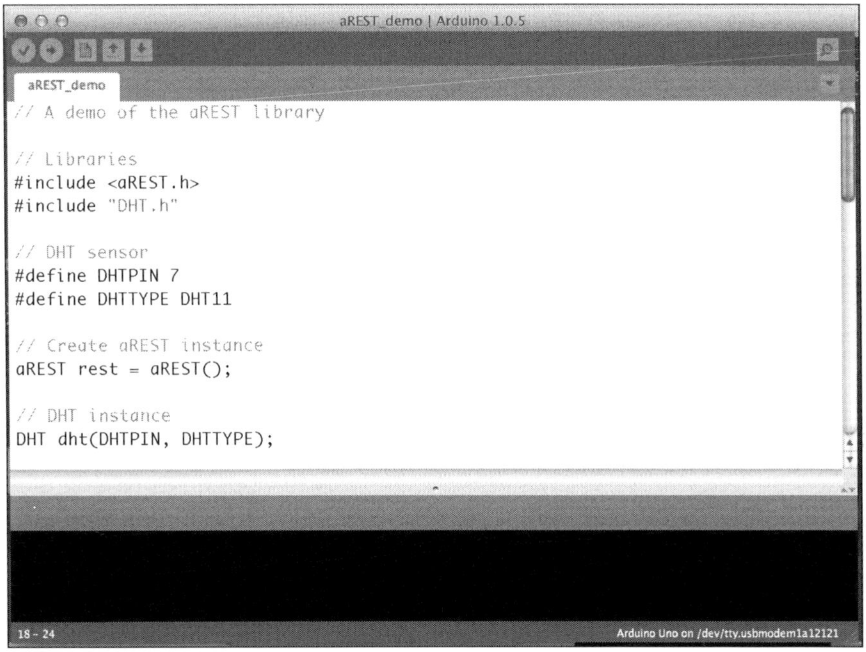

You will basically use two buttons that you can find on the left-hand side of the toolbar. The first one, with the check sign, can be use to compile the code. The second one will be used to upload the code to the Arduino board. Note that if the code has not been compiled yet, the upload button will also compile the code before uploading.

The second important window of the Arduino IDE is called the **serial monitor**. This is where you can monitor what your Arduino project is doing, using the `Serial.print()` statements in the code to generate debug output. You can access it by clicking on the top-right icon of the Arduino IDE main window.

The following screenshot shows what the serial monitor looks like:

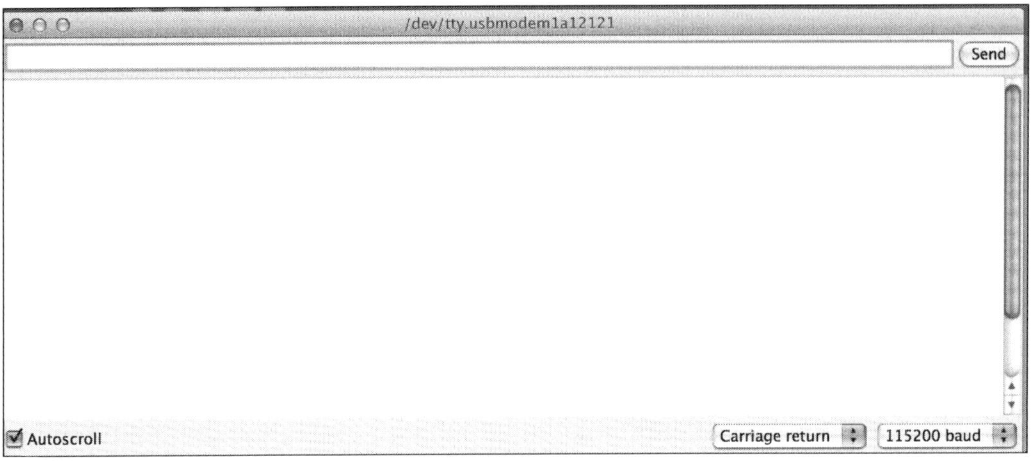

We are now going to build our first Arduino sketch in this book. What we want to achieve is simply to control the relay and read data from the DHT11 sensor. To do so, you are going to use the aREST library by sending commands from your computer. In the next chapter of this book, we are going to use the same commands but via a Bluetooth or Wi-Fi connection. The goal of this section is really to make you familiar with the commands of the aREST library.

The following code is the complete Arduino sketch for this part:

```
// Libraries
#include <aREST.h>
#include "DHT.h"

// DHT sensor
#define DHTPIN 7
#define DHTTYPE DHT11

// Create aREST instance
aREST rest = aREST();

// DHT instance
DHT dht(DHTPIN, DHTTYPE);

// Variables to be exposed to the API
int temperature;
int humidity;
```

```
void setup(void) {
  // Start Serial (with 115200 as the baud rate)
  Serial.begin(115200);

  // Expose variables to REST API
  rest.variable("temperature",&temperature);
  rest.variable("humidity",&humidity);

  // Give name and ID to device
  rest.set_id("001");
  rest.set_name("arduino_project");

  // Start temperature sensor
  dht.begin();

}

void loop() {

  // Measure from DHT
  float h = dht.readHumidity();
  float t = dht.readTemperature();

  temperature = (int)t;
  humidity = (int)h;

  // Handle REST calls
  rest.handle(Serial);

}
```

Let's explore the details of this Arduino sketch using the following steps:

1. The Arduino sketch starts by importing the required libraries for the project:

   ```
   #include <aREST.h>
   #include "DHT.h"
   ```

2. After that, we need to define on which pin the DHT11 sensor is connected to, and which is the type of the sensor:

   ```
   #define DHTPIN 7
   #define DHTTYPE DHT11
   ```

3. We also need to create an instance of the aREST library:

   ```
   aREST rest = aREST();
   ```

4. We also need to create an instance of the DHT11 sensor so that we can measure data from it:

   ```
   DHT dht(DHTPIN, DHTTYPE);
   ```

5. Finally, we need to create two variables that will contain our measurements:

   ```
   int temperature;
   int humidity;
   ```

6. In the `setup()` function of the sketch, we need to start the serial port:

   ```
   Serial.begin(115200);
   ```

7. Next, we need to expose our two measurement variables so that we can access them via the serial port using the aREST library. Note that we have to pass the reference to these variables, not their values, as shown in the following code:

   ```
   rest.variable("temperature",&temperature);
   rest.variable("humidity",&humidity);
   ```

8. We also set an ID and name to our project. This will not play any role here, but is simply to identify our board in case we have many of them:

   ```
   rest.set_id("001");
   rest.set_name("arduino_project");
   ```

9. Finally, we start the DHT11 sensor:

   ```
   dht.begin();
   ```

10. Now, in the `loop()` function of the sketch, we make the measurements from the DHT11 sensor, and convert these measurements to integers (which is called "casting" in C):

    ```
    float h = dht.readHumidity();
    float t = dht.readTemperature();

    temperature = (int)t;
    humidity = (int)h;
    ```

11. Note that here we are converting these numbers into integers because it is the only variable type supported by the aREST library. However, as the resolution of the DHT11 sensor is limited, we are not losing any information here. Finally, we handle any requests coming from the outside using the following code:

    ```
    rest.handle(Serial);
    ```

> Note that all the code for this chapter can be found in the GitHub repository of the book at the following link:
>
> `https://github.com/marcoschwartz/arduino-android-blueprints`

It's now time to upload the sketch to your Arduino board. If you have any error when compiling, make sure that you installed all the required Arduino libraries for this chapter.

When this is done, simply open the serial monitor (making sure the serial speed is set to `115200`). Note that you could do the same with your own serial terminal software, for example, CoolTerm found at `http://freeware.the-meiers.org/`.

Now, we are going to test that the aREST library is working correctly. Let's proceed with the following steps:

1. First, we are going to query the board for its ID and name. To do so, type the following:

   ```
   /id
   ```

2. You should be greeted by the following answer:

   ```
   {"id": "001", "name": "arduino_project", "connected": true}
   ```

3. We are now going to see how to control the relay, as this is something we are going to do several times in this book. First, we need to define that the relay pin, which is pin number 8 of the Arduino board, is an output. To do so, we can simply type:

   ```
   /mode/8/o
   ```

4. You should receive the following answer on the serial monitor:

   ```
   {"message": "Pin D8 set to output", "id": "001", "name": "arduino_
   project", "connected": true}
   ```

5. Now, to activate the relay, we need to set the pin 8 to a `HIGH` state. This is done the following command:

   ```
   /digital/8/1
   ```

6. You should instantly receive a confirmation message, and hear the relay click. To switch the relay off again, simply type the following code:

   ```
   /digital/8/0
   ```

7. Now, we are going to read data from the board using the aREST library. For example, to read the temperature variable, you can simply type the following code:

   ```
   /temperature
   ```

8. You will receive the following confirmation message with the value of the temperature:

   ```
   {"temperature": 28, "id": "001", "name": "arduino_project",
   "connected": true}
   ```

9. You can do the same for humidity:

   ```
   /humidity
   ```

10. You will receive a similar message back:

    ```
    {"humidity": 35, "id": "001", "name": "arduino_project",
    "connected": true}
    ```

If this is working, congratulations! You now know the basics of the aREST library that we will use throughout the book. Note that for now we are using these commands via serial communications, but later in the book, we will first use the same commands via Bluetooth, and then via Wi-Fi to command the Arduino board from an Android device.

Now that we have seen how the aREST library is working, we are going to create our first Android project. Note that in this introductory chapter, we won't connect both together; this will be done in the next chapter of the book.

Creating your first Android project

In order to get started in the world of Android application projects, it would be very useful to set up a very basic project that goes through the two main processes in Android application development: coding the application and then testing it on an Android physical device.

> **Downloading the example code**
>
> You can download the example code files for all Packt books you have purchased from your account at `http://www.packtpub.com`. If you purchased this book elsewhere, you can visit `http://www.packtpub.com/support` and register to have the files e-mailed directly to you.

Setting up your first Hello Arduino project

Click on **New Project** when Android Studio launches as shown in the following screenshot:

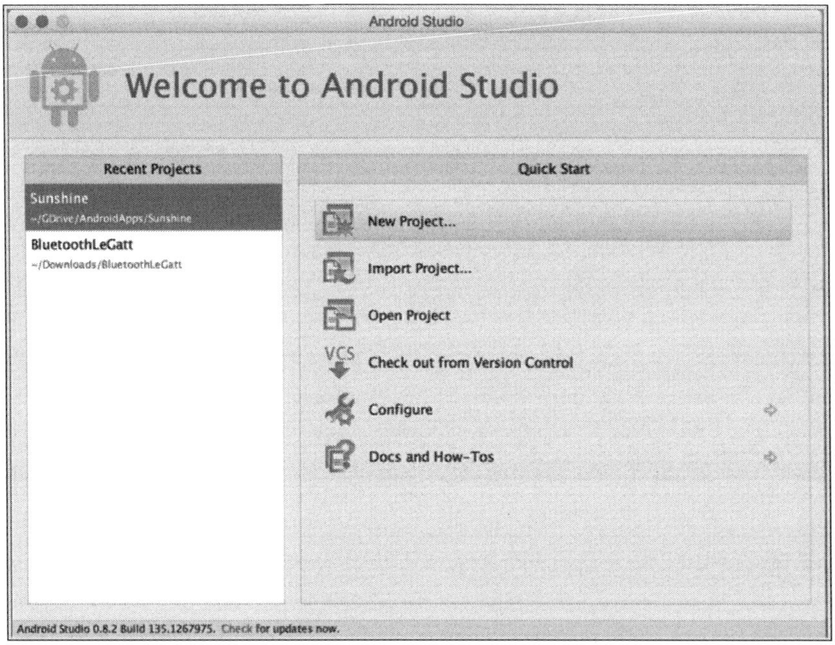

An important step within Android application development is configuring your project. This project will be using Android 4.3 as the minimum target SDK, since we intend to use the **Bluetooth Low Energy API**, which was introduced in this particular version of Android. In this case, we will name the project `Hello Arduino` and write down your company domain, as the convention for application package names is the reverse of your chosen domain.

Refer to the following screenshot:

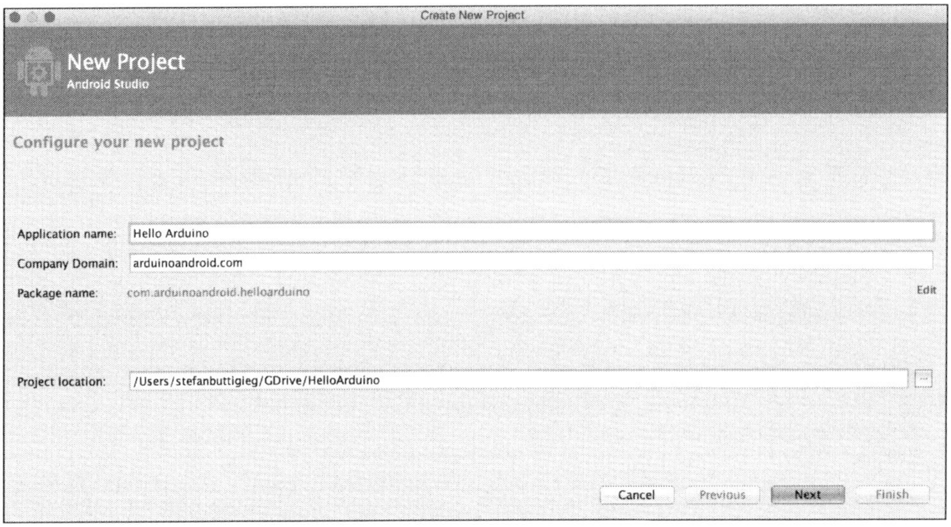

For the purposes of this particular project, we will go ahead and choose the most basic project, **Blank Activity**, as shown in the following screenshot. The other choices provide added functionality that we do not need at this stage.

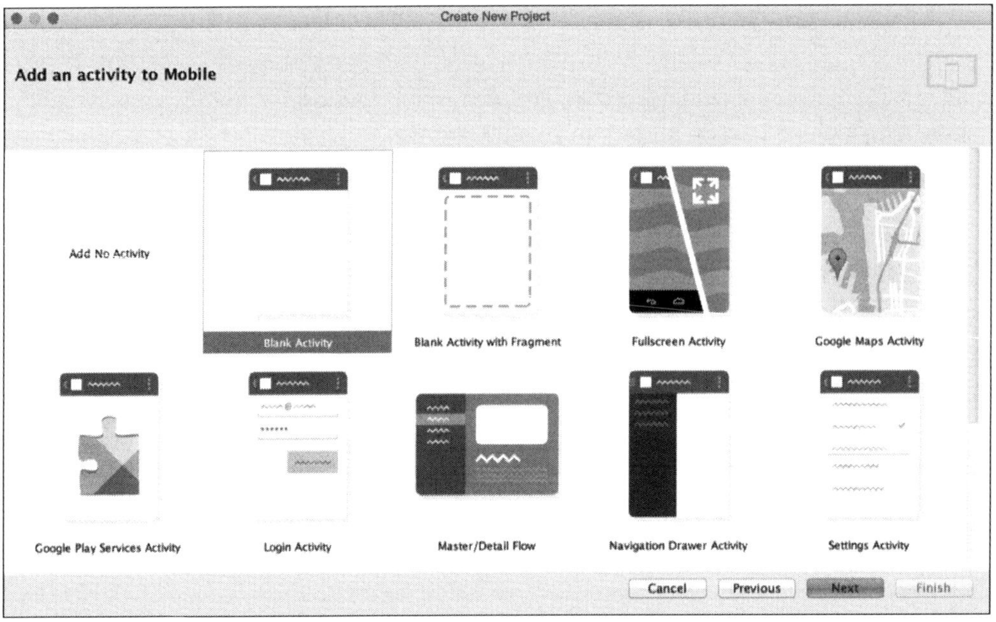

In the following screenshot, we choose **Blank Activity**, and we need to give a name to our main Java file. Let's keep it as `MyActivity`:

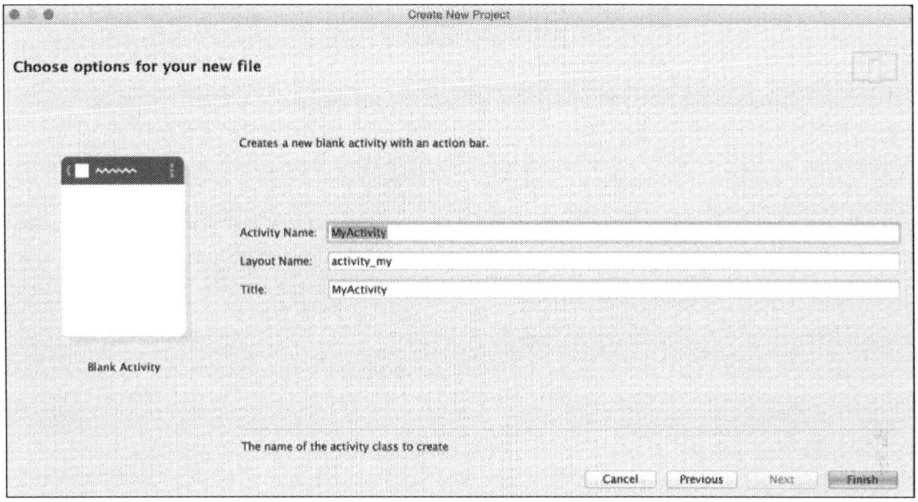

Once you follow through all the previous steps, you will be welcomed to this workspace, which gives a good overview of the project tree, main code editor, and the device that shows a preview of the **User Interface** (**UI**), as shown in the following screenshot:

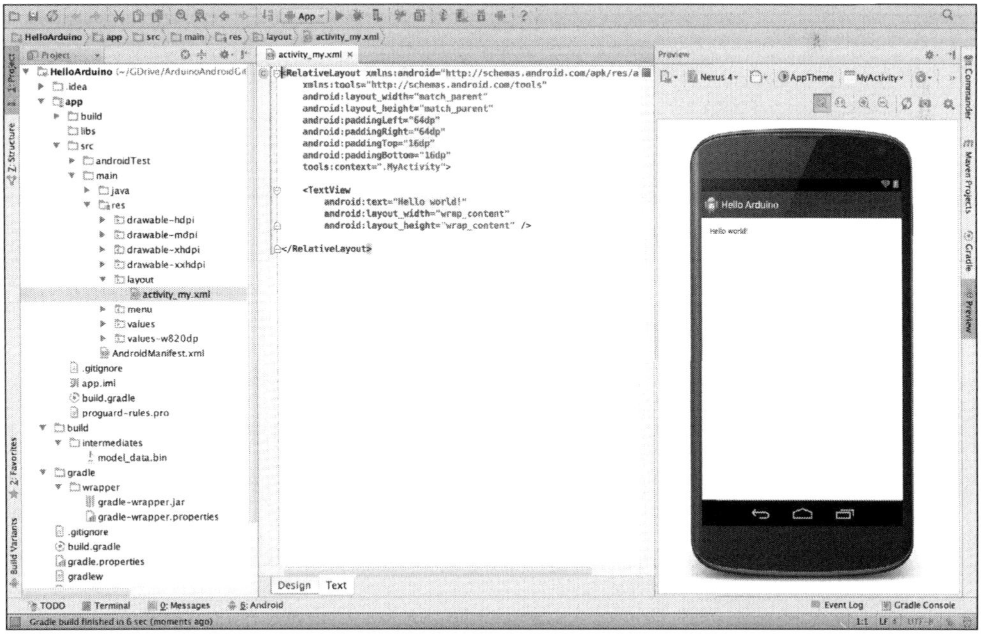

In this particular project, there will be no need to modify the existing code and therefore we will proceed with building our app and launching it on our physical Android device.

Installing your app on your physical device

Previously, we have connected and enabled our physical Android device via a USB. Within Android Studio, we need to set up the configuration to run our Android application.

This is done by choosing **Editing Configurations** from the main toolbar as shown in the following screenshot:

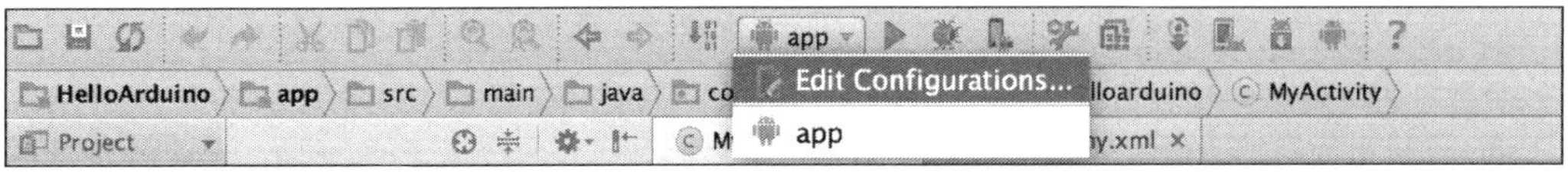

In the **Editing Configurations** window, we will click on the + sign and choose **Android Application** where we set up the configuration with the following settings and confirm them by pressing **OK**:

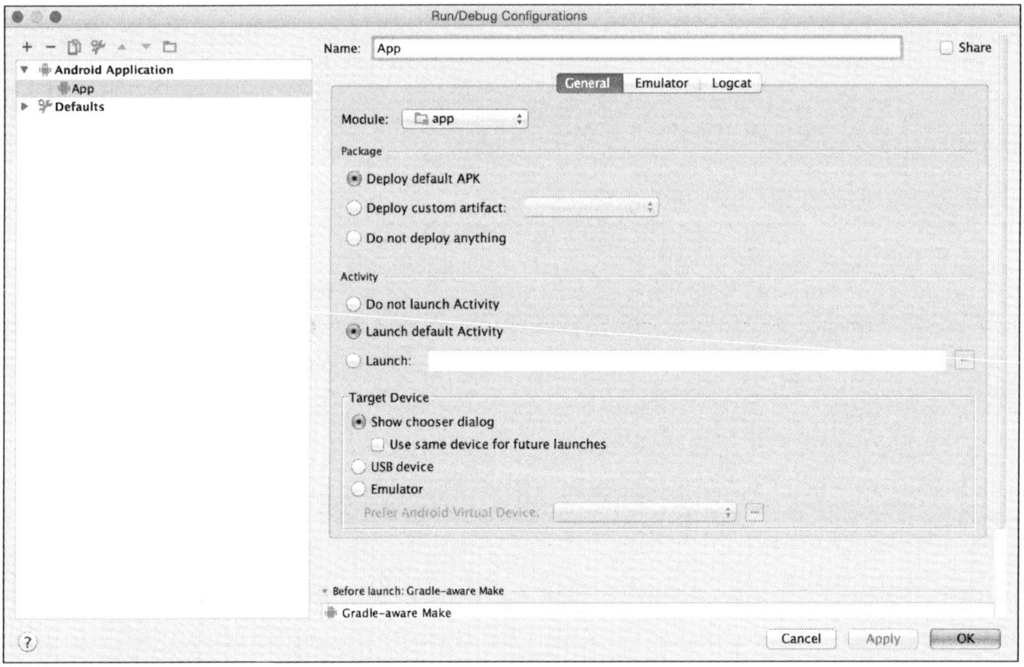

After setting up everything, we are ready to run the app. Choose the **App** configuration, which we previously set up, and press the **Play** button (green triangle) as shown in the following screenshot:

There is the possibility of creating an **Android Virtual Device** (**AVD**) to install the application. However, at this point in time, there are no virtual emulators that support Bluetooth, which we will need for a number of projects in this book. So, we will focus on setting up your Android physical device running Android 4.3 or higher.

In the next step, choose your physical device and press **OK**, as shown in the following screenshot:

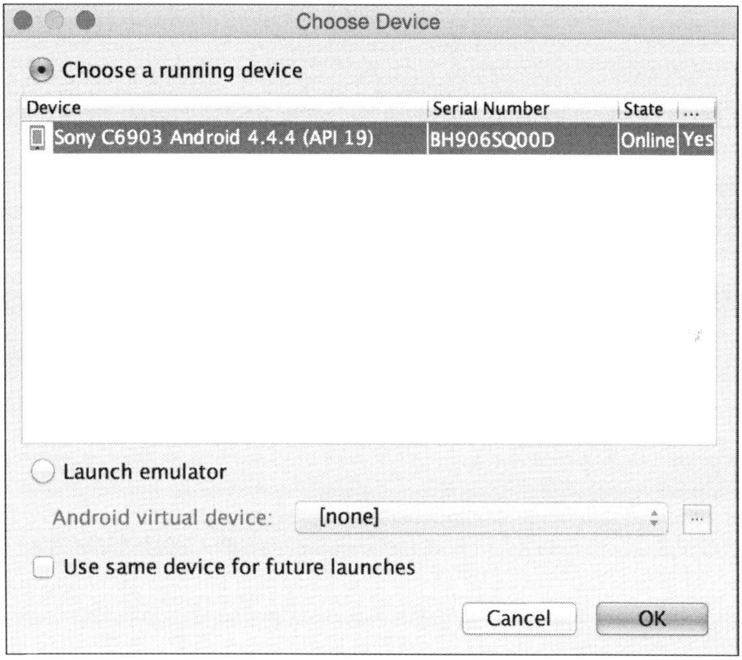

You should expect the following to show up on your Android device if you have set up everything in the correct manner:

Summary

Let's summarize what we did in this chapter of the book. We built a very simple Arduino project comprising an Arduino board, a relay module, and a temperature and humidity sensor. We saw how to connect these components together so that we can control the relay as an output and read data from the sensor. We also saw the basics of the aREST library, which we will use in the whole book to control the Arduino board from an Android device.

On the Android side, we have prepared our IDE and Android device for development, which will prepare us for the upcoming projects that we have prepared for you in this book and help us have a seamless experience. We also had the opportunity to compile our first app and get it up and running on our Android device.

At this stage, you can already repeat the steps we took in this chapter to really get familiar with the Arduino IDE, the commands of the aREST library, and the Android development environment. We will use these tools extensively in the rest of this book; so, it is crucial that are you familiar with them.

2

Controlling an Arduino Board via Bluetooth

This second chapter of the book will be about putting things together and writing our first app to control an Arduino board via **Bluetooth Low Energy** (**BLE**). We chose to use BLE for all the Bluetooth projects of this book as it is the latest standard for Bluetooth communication at the time of publication. Compared to previous Bluetooth modules, BLE modules have low energy consumption as the standard works in bursts rather than maintaining a persistent connection. In addition, BLE offers low latency and has a comparable range to the older Bluetooth standards.

We will connect a BLE module to Arduino as well as an LED that we will control via an Android app. Then, we will write an Arduino sketch that uses the aREST library so that we can receive commands via Bluetooth coming from a smartphone or tablet.

The Android app will also be able to control the board remotely and we will have the opportunity to enhance the user experience by learning how to include buttons to switch the LED on and off.

The following will be the main takeaways from this chapter:

- Connecting a BLE module to an Arduino board
- Writing an Arduino sketch to enable Bluetooth communications on the Arduino board
- Writing an Android application to send commands to the Arduino board via Bluetooth

Hardware and software requirements

The first thing you will need for this project is an Arduino Uno board.

Then, you will need a BLE module. We chose the Adafruit nRF8001 chip because it comes with a nice Arduino library, and it already has existing examples of Android apps to control the module.

The following is a close-up picture of the module we used for this project:

You will also need one LED of the color of your choice, and a 330 Ohm resistor. Finally, to make the different electrical connections, you will also need a breadboard and some jumper wires.

The following is the list of all hardware parts you will need for this project, along with links to find these parts on the Web:

- The Arduino Uno board (`http://www.adafruit.com/product/50`)
- LEDs (`https://www.sparkfun.com/products/9590`)
- The 330 Ohm resistor (`https://www.sparkfun.com/products/8377`)
- The Adafruit nRF8001 breakout board (`https://www.adafruit.com/products/1697`)
- The breadboard (`https://www.adafruit.com/product/64`)
- Jumper wires (`https://www.adafruit.com/product/758`)

On the software side, you will need the following:

- The Arduino IDE (`http://arduino.cc/en/Main/Software`)
- The Arduino aREST library (`https://github.com/marcoschwartz/aREST/`)
- The nRF8001 Arduino library for the BLE chip (`https://github.com/adafruit/Adafruit_nRF8001`)

To install a given library, simply extract the folder in your `Arduino /libraries` folder (or create this folder if it doesn't exist yet). To find your `Arduino` folder or define a new one, you can go to the **Preferences** option of the Arduino IDE.

Configuring the hardware

We will now build the hardware part of the project. To help you out, the following is a schematic of the project:

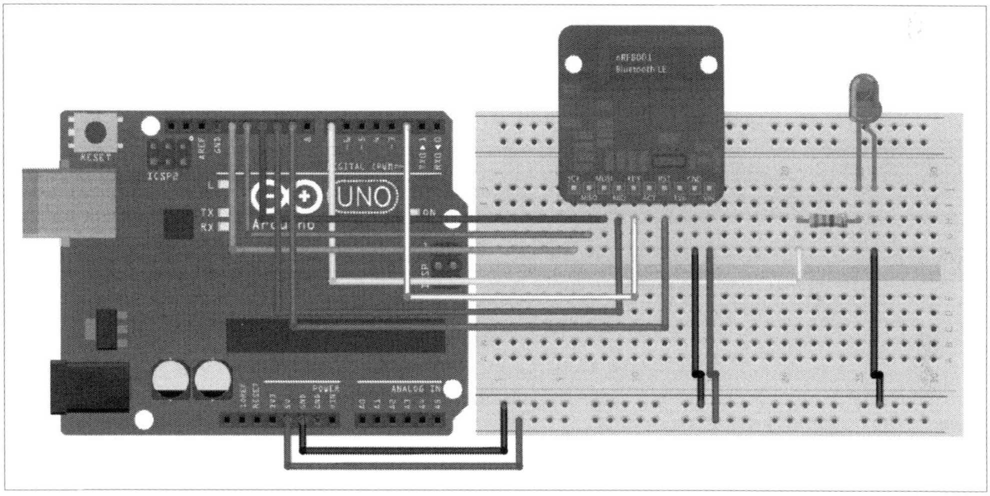

Now, we will perform the following steps:

1. The first step is to place the Bluetooth module and the LED on the breadboard.
2. Then, connect the power supply from the Arduino board to the breadboard: 5V of the Arduino board goes to the red power rail, and **GND** goes to the blue power rail.
3. We will now connect the BLE module. First, connect the power supply of the module: **GND** goes to the blue power rail, and **VIN** goes to the red power rail.

4. After this, you need to connect the different wires responsible for the **Serial Peripheral Interface** (**SPI**) communications: **SCK** to Arduino pin **13**, **MISO** to Arduino pin **12**, and **MOSI** to Arduino pin **11**.
5. Then, connect the **REQ** pin to Arduino pin **10**. Finally, connect the **RDY** pin to Arduino pin **2**, and the **RST** pin to Arduino pin **9**.
6. For the LED, simply place the resistor on the breadboard so it is in series with the LED, connected to the anode of the LED, which is the longest pin of the LED.
7. Then, connect the other side of the resistor to Arduino pin **7**.
8. Finally, connect the other pin of the LED (the cathode) to the blue power rail, that is to the ground.

This is an image of the completely assembled project:

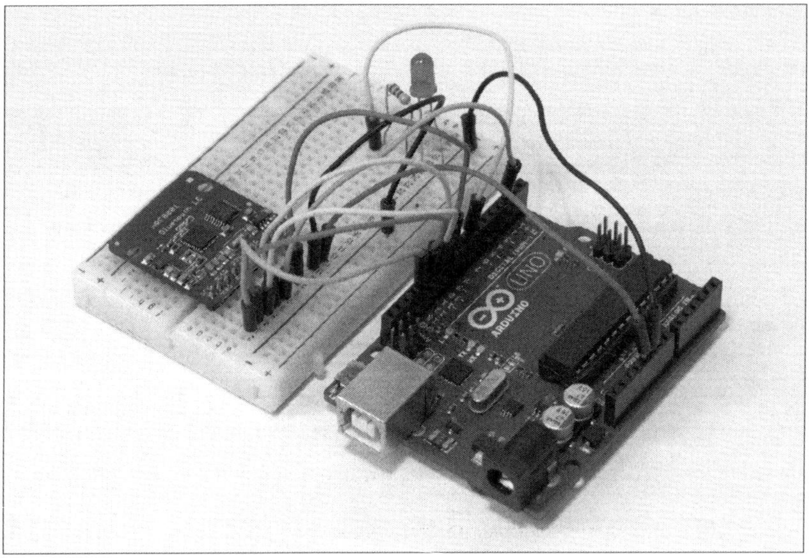

Writing the Arduino sketch

We will now write the Arduino sketch so that the Arduino board can talk with the BLE module and receive commands from Android via Bluetooth. Here is the complete sketch for this part:

```
#define LIGHTWEIGHT 1

#include <SPI.h>
#include "Adafruit_BLE_UART.h"
```

```
#include <aREST.h>

// Pins
#define ADAFRUITBLE_REQ 10
#define ADAFRUITBLE_RDY 2     // This should be an interrupt pin, //
on Uno thats #2 or #3
#define ADAFRUITBLE_RST 9

// Create aREST instance
aREST rest = aREST();

// BLE instance
Adafruit_BLE_UART BTLEserial = Adafruit_BLE_UART(ADAFRUITBLE_REQ,
ADAFRUITBLE_RDY, ADAFRUITBLE_RST);

void setup(void)
{
  // Start Serial
  Serial.begin(9600);
  Serial.println(F("Adafruit Bluefruit Low Energy nRF8001 Print echo
demo"));

  // Start BLE
  BTLEserial.begin();

  // Give name and ID to device
  rest.set_id("001");
  rest.set_name("my_arduino");
}

aci_evt_opcode_t laststatus = ACI_EVT_DISCONNECTED;

void loop() {

  // Tell the nRF8001 to do whatever it should be working on.
  BTLEserial.pollACI();

  // Ask what is our current status
  aci_evt_opcode_t status = BTLEserial.getState();
  // If the status changed....
  if (status != laststatus) {
    // print it out!
    if (status == ACI_EVT_DEVICE_STARTED) {
        Serial.println(F("* Advertising started"));
```

```
        }
        if (status == ACI_EVT_CONNECTED) {
            Serial.println(F("* Connected!"));
        }
        if (status == ACI_EVT_DISCONNECTED) {
            Serial.println(F("* Disconnected or advertising timed out"));
        }
        // OK set the last status change to this one
        laststatus = status;
      }

      // Handle REST calls
      if (status == ACI_EVT_CONNECTED) {
        rest.handle(BTLEserial);
      }
    }
```

Now, let's see the details of this sketch. It starts by importing the required libraries for the nRF8001 BLE module and the aREST library:

```
#include <SPI.h>
#include "Adafruit_BLE_UART.h"
#include <aREST.h>
```

We will also specify an option for the aREST library, called `LIGHTWEIGHT`. This means that the Arduino board will only return a limited amount of data back to the Android phone. It will return the value of a variable when we read from the board, and no data at all when we send a command to the board. This is required when using BLE communications. This is done with the following piece of code:

```
#define LIGHTWEIGHT 1
```

Then, we will define which pin the BLE module is connected to:

```
#define ADAFRUITBLE_REQ 10
#define ADAFRUITBLE_RDY 2     // This should be an interrupt pin, on
Uno thats #2 or #3
#define ADAFRUITBLE_RST 9
```

Note that we don't define the pins for the SPI pins of the BLE module, as they are already defined in the module's library.

After this, we can create an instance of the aREST API that will be used to handle the requests coming via Bluetooth:

```
aREST rest = aREST();
```

We also need to create an instance for the BLE module, with the pins we defined earlier:

```
Adafruit_BLE_UART BTLEserial = Adafruit_BLE_UART(ADAFRUITBLE_REQ,
ADAFRUITBLE_RDY, ADAFRUITBLE_RST);
```

Now, in the `setup()` function of the sketch, we will start the serial communications, and print a welcome message:

```
Serial.begin(9600);
Serial.println(F("Adafruit Bluefruit Low Energy nRF8001 Print echo
demo"));
```

Note that the welcome message is printed using the `F()` function around the message, which puts the string variable directly into the Arduino program memory. This is done to save some dynamic memory (RAM) for this sketch.

We will also initialize the BLE module:

```
BTLEserial.begin();
```

Finally, we will give an ID and a name to our board:

```
rest.set_id("001");
rest.set_name("my_arduino");
```

In the `loop()` function of the sketch, we will check the status of the BLE module:

```
BTLEserial.pollACI();
```

After this, we will get this status and store it in a variable:

```
aci_evt_opcode_t status = BTLEserial.getState();
```

If there is some device connected to our BLE module, we will then handle the incoming request using the aREST library:

```
if (status == ACI_EVT_CONNECTED) {
    rest.handle(BTLEserial);
  }
```

> Note that all the code for this chapter can be found inside the GitHub repository of the book at `https://github.com/marcoschwartz/arduino-android-blueprints`.

It's now time to upload the sketch to your Arduino board. When this is done, you can move on to the development of the Android app to control the Arduino board via the BLE sketch.

How to create a simple Android app to connect to the BLE module

Connecting the Adafruit BLE module will give us the opportunity to:

- Learn how to work with existing open source projects
- Analyze Java and understand how the `Main` activity connects to the layout files
- Modify the code to light up an LED via Bluetooth and get it to work

For this project, we will be using an open source project that works perfectly with our Adafruit Bluetooth module and is optimized for the Android Studio IDE. Throughout this chapter, we will also have the opportunity to explain what the different parts of the code are for.

To make the project work successfully, you need to make sure that you have installed the necessary SDKs outlined in *Chapter 1, Setting Up Your Workspace*. The SDK is available via SDK Manager, which is accessible by going to **Tools** > **Android** > **SDK Manager**.

The first step is to go to Tony Dicola's GitHub public repository, at `https://github.com/tdicola/BTLETest`, as shown in the following screenshot:

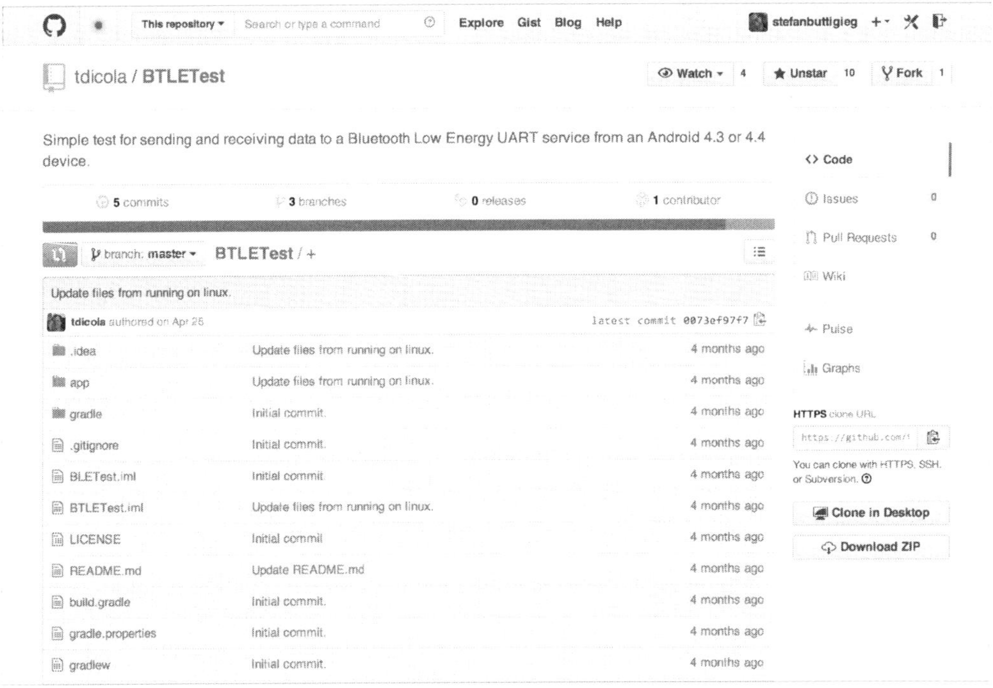

At this point, you can either opt to **Clone in Desktop** using the GitHub desktop application or download the ZIP file and extract the file to your desktop, as shown in the following screenshot:

Double-click on the extracted file (Windows and Mac).

Open Android Studio, then click on **Import Project** and **Choose Extracted Folder**, as shown here:

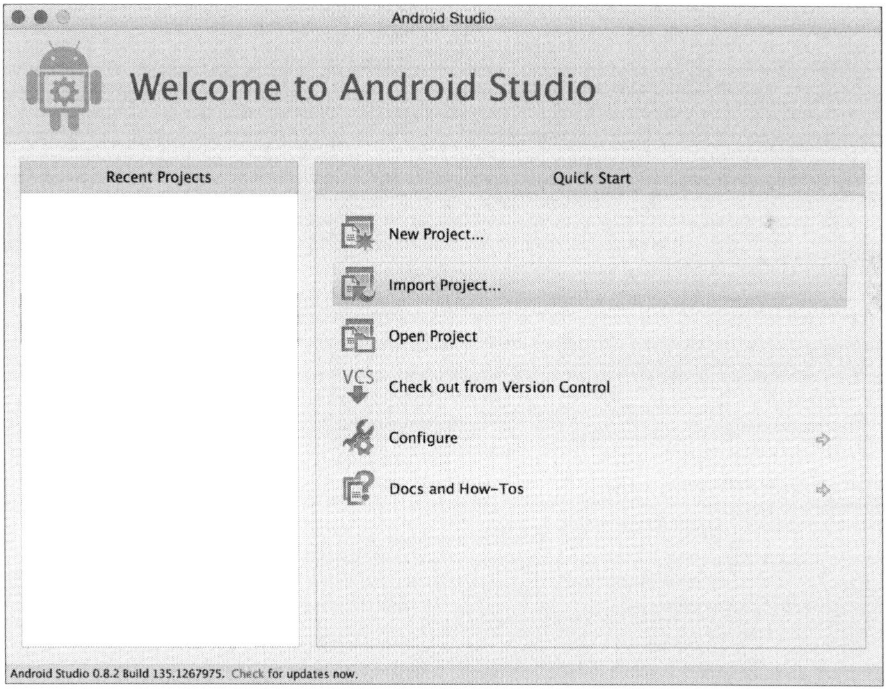

To aid you in the selection process, you will be able to see a small Android logo next to the folder you need to choose, as shown in the following screenshot:

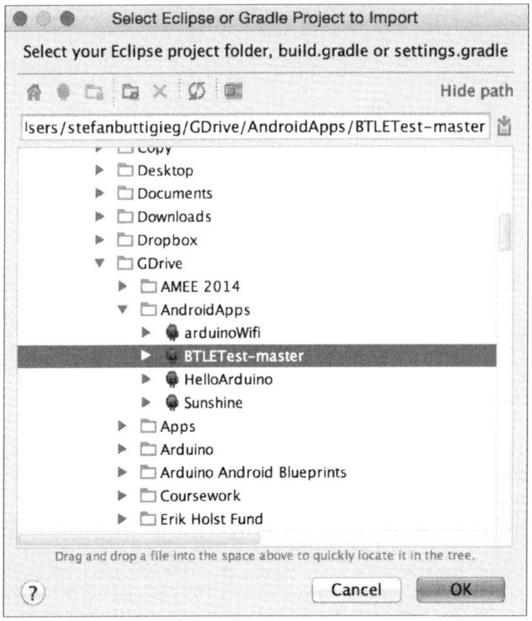

After successfully importing the project, you might need to modify the Gradle settings file so that it compiles correctly and is successfully built. The Gradle settings file acts as a preferences manager for our Android project and allows us to manage what libraries we would like to include for our project.

You can modify the Gradle settings file by accessing the project tree and clicking on **app > src** followed by **build.gradle**, as shown in the following screenshot :

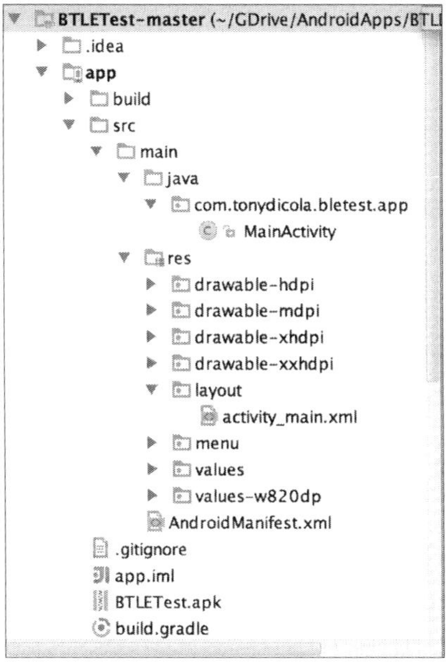

Our recommendation is to alter `buildToolsVersion` to `19.1.0`. Do not be confused by **app** showing up in the tabs. The correct settings can be seen as follows:

MainActivity.java
app
activity_main.xml
apply plugin: 'android'
android {
compileSdkVersion 19
buildToolsVersion "19.1.0"
defaultConfig {
minSdkVersion 18
targetSdkVersion 19
versionCode 1
versionName "1.0"
}
buildTypes {
release {
runProguard false
proguardFiles getDefaultProguardFile('proguard-android.txt'), 'proguard-rules.txt'
}
}
}
dependencies {
compile fileTree(dir: 'libs', include: ['*.jar'])
}

Once you modify the settings in the Gradle **Settings** option, you will be asked to sync your project settings, and you will be able to do that by clicking on **Sync Now**. Once the Gradle settings file is set up, you can go ahead and test the app on your physical Android device that supports BLE (the device should be running Android 4.3 or higher). Run the app by going to the toolbar, clicking on **Run**, and selecting **Run app**, followed by choosing the right physical device, as shown in the following screenshot:

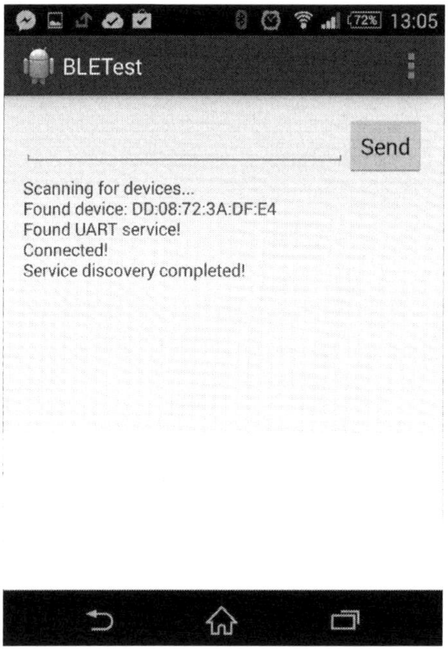

You can send out the following messages to the Bluetooth module by tapping on the **Text Field** and then tapping on **Send**:

- /mode/7/o /
- /digital/7/1 /
- /digital/7/0 /

When you see that the preceding messages respond with the right responses via the LED, which will switch on and switch off if you follow the previous order, we will then proceed to modifying the layout file.

Modifying the Android layout file

Modification of the Android layout file will simplify the user experience and allow us to switch the LED on and off with the tap of a button. In the Android layout file, we will add buttons for the following:

- Activating the pin to accept inputs
- Switch on LED
- Switch off LED

Go to the project tree, as shown in the following screenshot and follow this path: `app` > `src` > `res` > `layout` > `activity_main.xml`. Double-click on the `activity_main.xml` file.

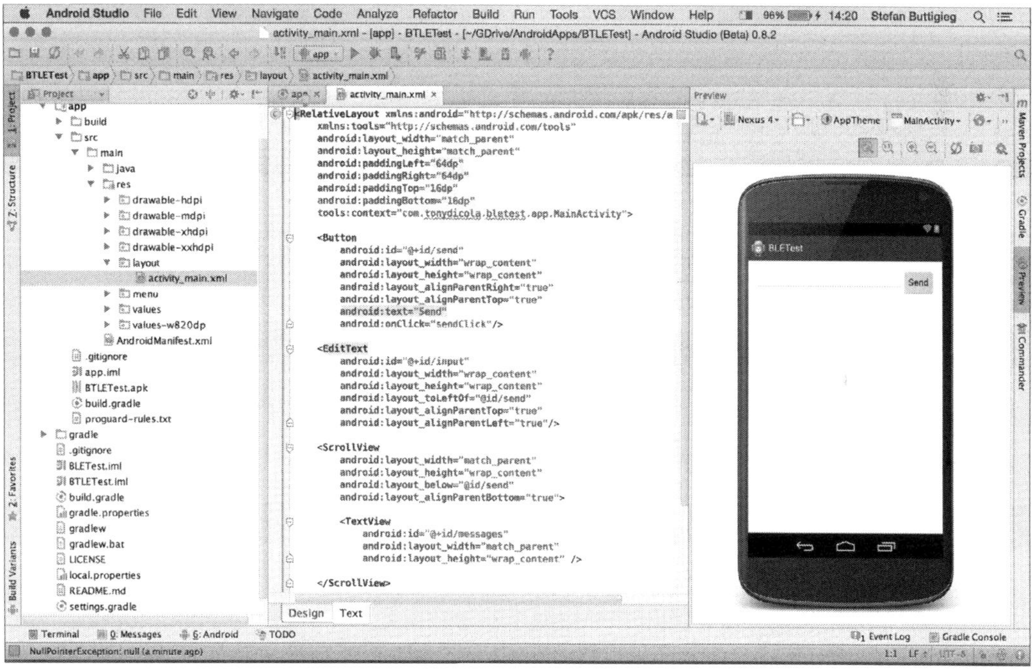

The Android layout files are managed either via the design view or via the text view, where the dimensions and properties are set using the XML format. In this particular case, we will stick to modifying the layout using the design view, as shown in the following screenshot:

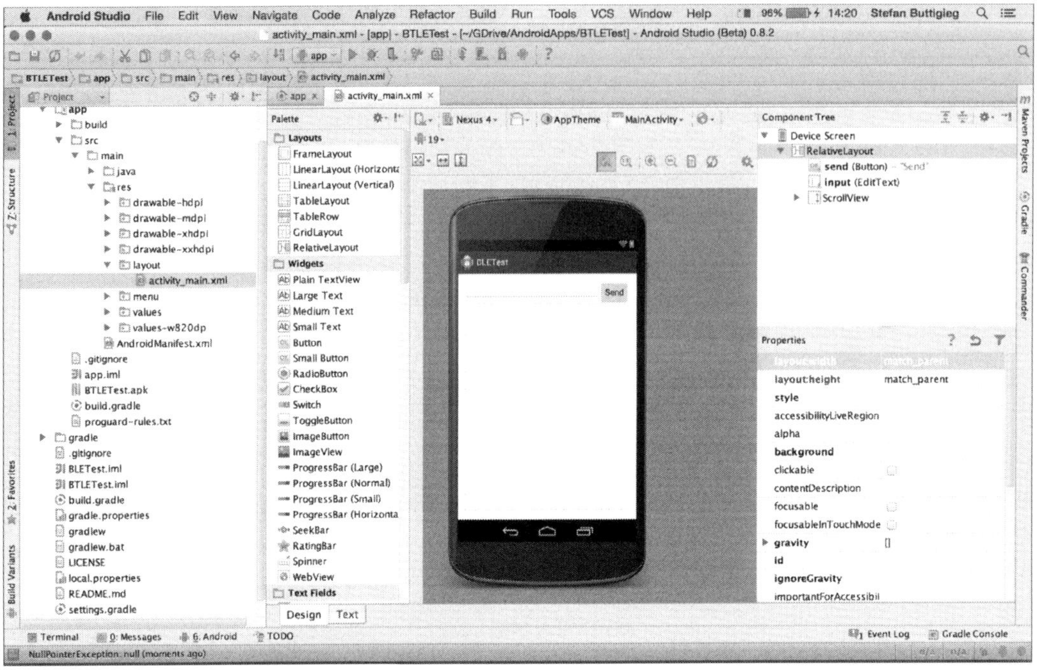

Within the design view, there is a palette with defined user-interface elements that the developer can use to drag-and-drop into the design view and create customized layouts. To follow proper design-develop-distribute methodology, we will start off by creating a paper prototype of how we would like the app to look and work out, as shown in the following screenshot. At this point of time, our paper prototypes will be neither sophisticated nor adherent to design principles, but we would like to help you get used to the process to enable you to design high-quality apps.

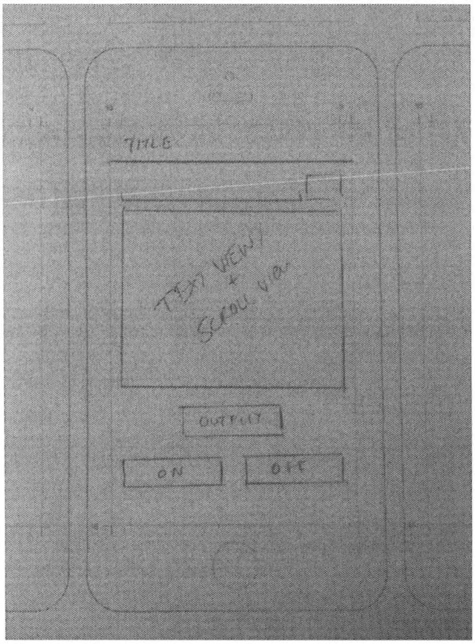

Having this paper prototype as our guide, we can then start modifying the design. We will start off by resizing the **Scroll View** area, which shows the response that the Android physical device receives when connecting with the BLE module. This will allow us to visualize how we would like to design the layout.

Adding buttons to the interface is as easy as dragging and dropping buttons from the **Palette** option to the user interface. The **Palette** option is available on the left-hand side of the design view. In this case, we will add the following three buttons:

- Set output
- Switch on
- Switch off

If you double-click on the button that you've included in the interface, you will be able to change the text and ID. Standard Java naming conventions recommend the use of the camel-case naming convention; thus, you should identify them as follows:

- The **Set Output** button
  - **Text**: `Set Output`
  - **ID**: `setOutputBtn`

- The **Switch On** button
  - **Text**: `Switch On LED`
  - **ID**: `switchOnBtn`
- The **Set Output** button
  - **Text**: `Switch Off LED`
  - **ID**: `switchOffBtn`

With the layout setup, we can proceed to connecting the layout to our main activity code.

Connecting the modified layout to the corresponding activity

From the project tree, follow the path: `app` > `src` > `main` > `java` > `com.tonydicola.bletest.app` > `MainActivity`, as shown in the following screenshot:

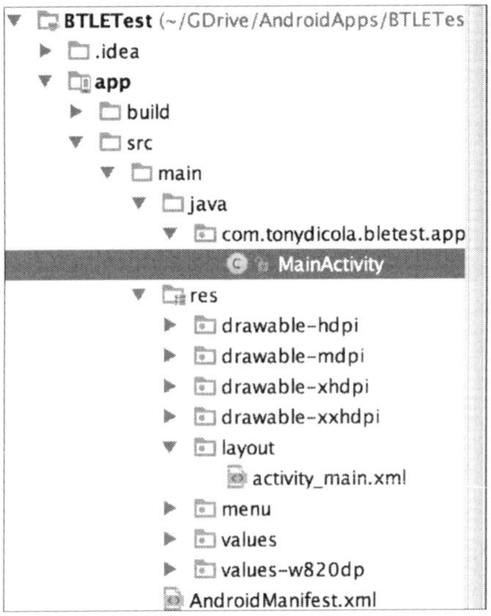

Double-click on `MainActivity.java`. The screen for `MainActivity.java` will look as follows. In the following paragraphs, we will have an opportunity to go through the code and understand what role it plays within the app. There are a number of comments within the code (statements starting with //////) that will further explain the role of those lines of code.

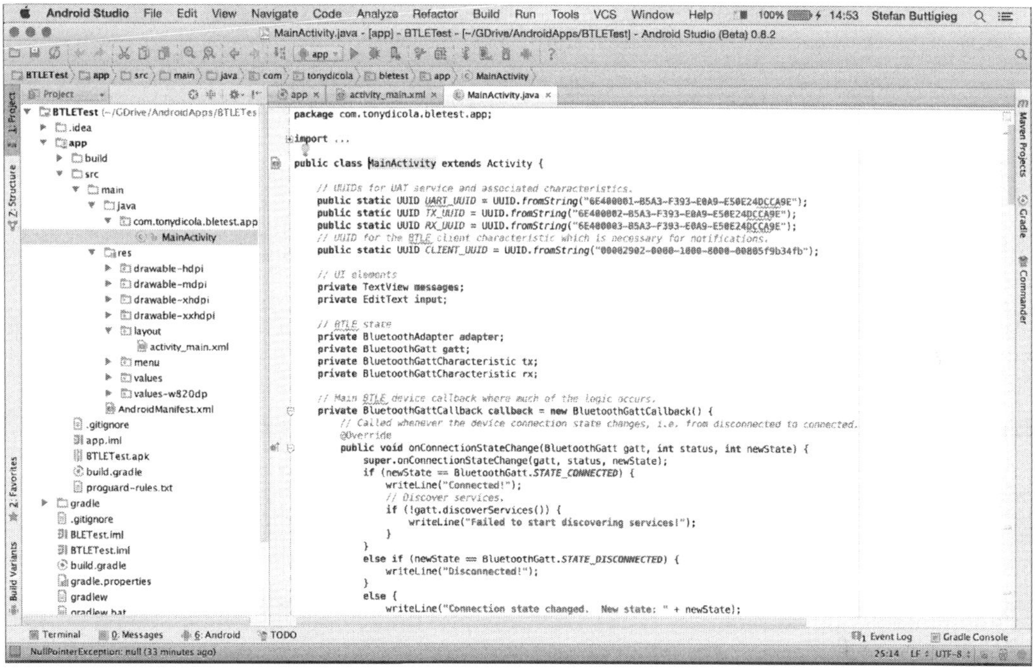

If we quickly analyze the code, we can see the following structure:

- The package name.
- An import statement.
- Declaration of private and public variables (which can be used throughout the whole activity).
- `BluetoothGattCallback`: This is the method that deals with the callback and where much of the logic takes place.
- `onServicesDiscovered`: This is the method that deals with Bluetooth service discovery.
- `onCharacteristicChanged`: This is the method that takes care of any change in characteristics.

- `onCreate`: This is the method that deals with the main layout and how it functions. The `onCreate` method is called when the activity is first shown, and plays a very important role in the Android app life cycle. Most of the code in this section will relate to the Android layout.
- `onResume` and `onStop`: These are the methods that form a part of the Android app life cycle and determine how the app will react at different points.
- `sendClick`: This is the method that deals with what processes will be run when the **Send** button is clicked.
- `parseIDs`: This is the method that will return the Bluetooth module's ID in string format.
- `Boilerplate`: This is the code that is available within the primary template when creating this project, but it is not necessarily relevant for it.

Understanding the code will help us to make the right modifications; we will start by declaring the UI elements as private variables by adding the following code:

```
private Button setoutput;
private Button switchon;
private Button switchoff;
```

We then proceed to the `onCreate` method, where we will add the code that will recognize the actual buttons within the layout and where we will also add the `onClickListener` method to each button, which allows the Android app to listen to any of the users' interactions with the button and act accordingly.

First, we will start off by grabbing references to the UI elements by adding the following code:

```
setoutput = (Button) findViewById(R.id.setToOutputBtn);
switchon = (Button) findViewById(R.id.switchOnBtn);
switchoff = (Button) findViewById(R.id.switchOffBtn);
```

Just after these references to the UI elements, we will add some more code, which will allow us to send the right messages to the BLE module and to switch on and switch off the light:

```
setoutput.setOnClickListener(new View.OnClickListener() {
            public void onClick(View v) {
                String setOutputMessage = "/mode/7/o /";
                tx.setValue(setOutputMessage.getBytes(Charset.
forName("UTF-8")));
```

```
                if (gatt.writeCharacteristic(tx)) {
                    writeLine("Sent: " + setOutputMessage);
                }
                else {
                    writeLine("Couldn't write TX characteristic!");
                }

            }
        });

        switchon.setOnClickListener(new View.OnClickListener() {
            public void onClick(View v) {
                String switchOnMessage = "/digital/7/1 /";
                tx.setValue(switchOnMessage.getBytes(Charset.
forName("UTF-8")));
                if (gatt.writeCharacteristic(tx)) {
                    writeLine("Sent: " + switchOnMessage);
                }
                else {
                    writeLine("Couldn't write TX characteristic!");
                }
            }
        });

        switchoff.setOnClickListener(new View.OnClickListener() {
            public void onClick(View v) {
                String switchOffMessage = "/digital/7/0 /";
                tx.setValue(switchOffMessage.getBytes(Charset.
forName("UTF-8")));
                if (gatt.writeCharacteristic(tx)) {
                    writeLine("Sent: " + switchOffMessage);
                }
                else {
                    writeLine("Couldn't write TX characteristic!");
                }
            }
        });
```

With the preceding methods implemented, we should now be able to build the app and test it on our physical device. The final result should look as follows:

You should now successfully be able to switch on and switch off the light from the Android app.

How to go further

There are several things you can do to go further with what you learned in this chapter. You can use what you learned to control more than just a simple LED. For example, you can connect the relay module we used in the first chapter and control it via Bluetooth. This already allows you to control much bigger devices, such as lamps, all via your Android phone. Of course, such projects require that you take safety precautions, which will be detailed in the chapter where we will build such an application.

You can also work on improving the Android application by improving the user interface and learning how to further modify the Android layout files with better-looking buttons, customized app icons, and general improvements to the user experience. As we go on in this book, we will have further opportunities to build on this code and enable more functions and capabilities.

Summary

Let's summarize what we learned in this chapter. We connected a BLE module to Arduino as well as a simple red LED that we controlled remotely. After this, we wrote a sketch that enabled the Arduino board to receive commands via the Bluetooth module.

On the Android side, we took the opportunity to take an existing project, analyze it, modify it, and run the final application on our physical Android device.

In the next chapter, we will build a wireless weather station using what we just learnt in this chapter. We will connect several sensors to an Arduino board, and read data coming from these sensors using an Android app communicating with the Arduino board via Bluetooth.

3
Bluetooth Weather Station

In this chapter, we will build the first complete application of this book using Arduino and Android. We will build a small weather station using Arduino, which will be accessed by an Android app via Bluetooth.

On the Arduino side, we will build a simple weather station using a temperature and humidity sensor along with an ambient light-level sensor. We will connect a **Bluetooth Low Energy** (**BLE**) module to the project so that the Android phone can access the measurements wirelessly.

We will develop a simple Android app with an interface that allows us to:

- Access all the measurements performed by the weather station with the tap of a button
- Display each measurement within an enlarged text view

Hardware and software requirements

The first thing you will need for this project is an Arduino Uno board.

Then, you need a BLE module. We chose the Adafruit nRF8001 chip because it comes with a nice Arduino library, and it already has existing examples of Android apps to control the module. This is the same module that we used in the previous chapter.

For the sensors, I chose a DHT11 sensor to measure the temperature and the ambient humidity. DHT11 is a digital temperature and humidity sensor that is really easy to integrate with Arduino. There are several solutions available for Arduino, but this sensor was chosen because it is one of the easiest to interface with Arduino. To make the sensor work with Arduino, we will also need a 4.7K Ohm resistor.

We will also use a photocell in series with a 10K Ohm resistor to measure the ambient light level. The photocell is basically a resistor that will change its resistance depending on the incoming light on the cell. It will be connected to the Arduino analog input to measure the ambient light level.

Finally, you will need a breadboard and some jumper wires to make the different connections.

The following is a list of all hardware parts you will need for this project, along with links to find these parts on the Web:

- The Arduino Uno board (`http://www.adafruit.com/product/50`)
- The DHT11 sensor and 4.7K Ohm resistor (`https://www.adafruit.com/products/386`)
- The photocell (`https://www.sparkfun.com/products/9088`)
- The 10K Ohm resistor (`https://www.sparkfun.com/products/8374`)
- Adafruit nRF8001 breakout board (`https://www.adafruit.com/products/1697`)
- The breadboard (`https://www.adafruit.com/product/64`)
- Jumper wires (`https://www.adafruit.com/product/758`)

On the software side, you will need the Arduino IDE as usual, and the Arduino aREST library, which is found at `https://github.com/marcoschwartz/aREST/`.

The photocell make measurements from the DHT11 sensor, you will need the DHT library found at `https://github.com/adafruit/DHT-sensor-library`.

For the BLE chip, you will also need the nRF8001 Arduino library found at `https://github.com/adafruit/Adafruit_nRF8001`.

To install a given library, simply extract the folder in your `Arduino /libraries` folder (or create this folder if it doesn't exist yet).

Hardware configuration

We will now build the hardware for this project. To help you out, here is a schematic of the project:

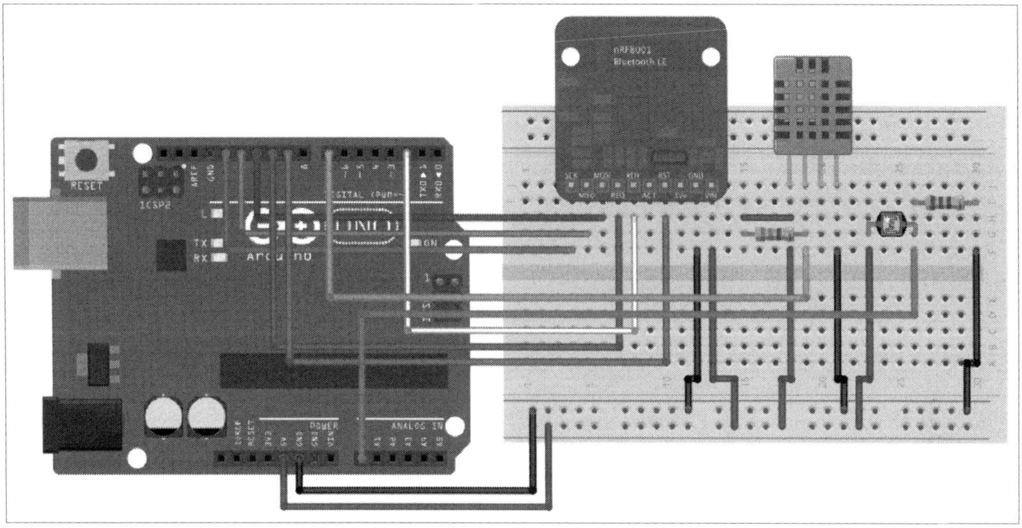

Now, we will perform the following steps:

1. The first step is to place the Bluetooth module, the DHT11 sensor, and the photocell on the breadboard.
2. Then, connect the power supply from the Arduino board to the breadboard: 5V of the Arduino board goes to the red power rail, and **GND** goes to the blue power rail.
3. We will now connect the BLE module. First, connect the power supply of the module: **GND** goes to the blue power rail, and **VIN** goes to the red power rail.
4. After that, you need to connect the different wires responsible for the SPI interface: **SCK** to Arduino pin **13**, **MISO** to Arduino pin **12**, and **MOSI** to Arduino pin **11**.

5. Then, connect the **REQ** pin to Arduino pin **10**. Finally, connect the **RDY** pin to Arduino pin **2**, and the **RST** pin to Arduino pin **9**.

   For the DHT sensor, this is the function of each pin on the sensor:

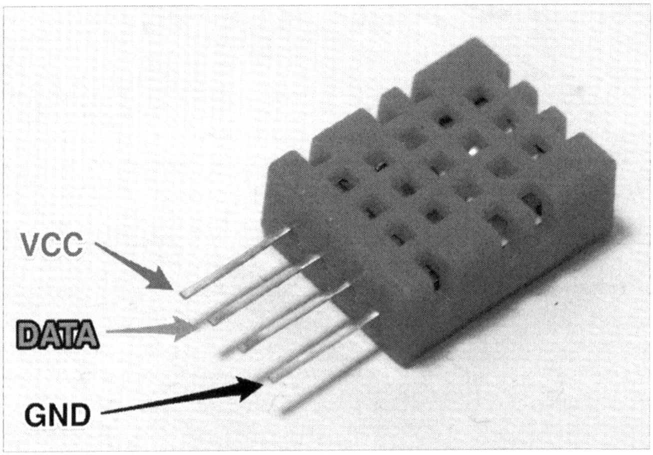

6. You need to first connect the power supply: the **VCC** pin goes to the red power rail on the breadboard, and the **GND** pin goes to the blue power rail.
7. You also need to connect the **DATA** pin to pin number **7** of the Arduino board.
8. Finally, place the 4.7K Ohm resistor between the **VCC** and the **DATA** pin of the sensor.
9. For the photocell, connect the 10K Ohm resistor in series with the photocell. This means that one pin of the photocell should be in contact (on the same row on the breadboard) with one pin of the resistor.
10. Then, connect the other pin of the resistor to the blue power rail, and the other pin of the photocell to the red power rail of the breadboard.

11. Finally, connect the common pin between the photocell and resistor to the analog pin **A0** of the Arduino board.

    This is an image of the completely assembled project:

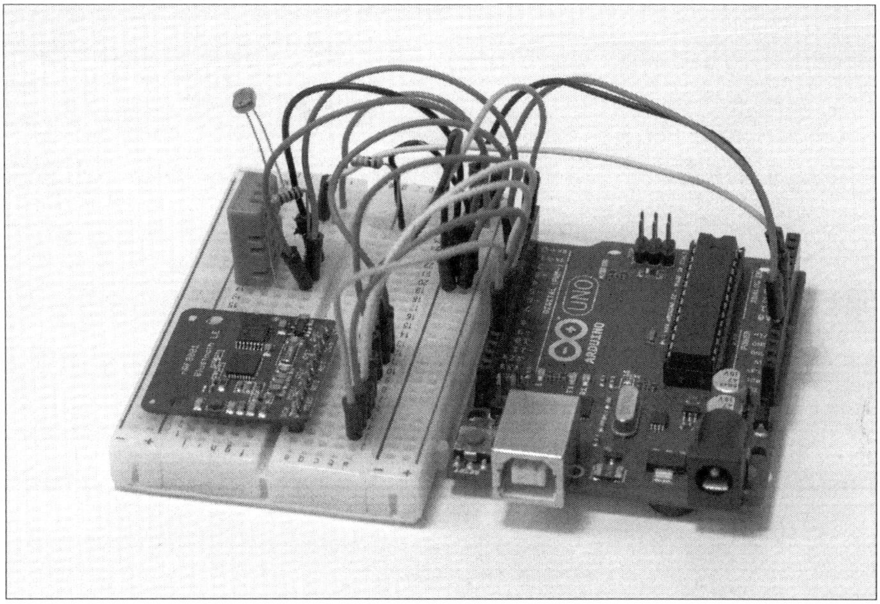

Testing the sensors

We will now write a simple Arduino sketch to test all the sensors of the project. This will ensure that all the connections were made correctly before writing our Android app using Bluetooth. This is the complete sketch for testing the sensors:

```
#include "DHT.h"

// DHT sensor
#define DHTPIN 7
#define DHTTYPE DHT11

// DHT instance
DHT dht(DHTPIN, DHTTYPE);

void setup()
{
  // Initialize the Serial port
  Serial.begin(9600);
```

```
    // Init DHT
    dht.begin();
  }

  void loop()
  {
    // Measure from DHT
    float temperature = dht.readTemperature();
    float humidity = dht.readHumidity();

    // Measure light level
    float sensor_reading = analogRead(A0);
    float light = sensor_reading/1024*100;

    // Display temperature
    Serial.print("Temperature: ");
    Serial.print((int)temperature);
    Serial.println(" C");

     // Display humidity
    Serial.print("Humidity: ");
    Serial.print(humidity);
    Serial.println("%");

    // Display light level
    Serial.print("Light: ");
    Serial.print(light);
    Serial.println("%");
    Serial.println("");

    // Wait 500 ms
    delay(500);

  }
```

Let's now look at this sketch in more detail. It starts by including the DHT11 library:

```
#include "DHT.h"
```

We also declare that the sensor is attached to pin number 7, and that the DHT sensor we are using is a DHT11 sensor by declaring constants:

```
#define DHTPIN 7

#define DHTTYPE DHT11
```

After that, we can declare an instance of the DHT sensor:

```
DHT dht(DHTPIN, DHTTYPE);
```

In the `setup()` function of the sketch, we will start the serial communications:

```
Serial.begin(9600);
```

We will also initialize the DHT sensor:

```
dht.begin();
```

In the `loop()` function of the sketch, we will perform the temperature and humidity measurements from the sensor:

```
float temperature = dht.readTemperature();
float humidity = dht.readHumidity();
```

We will also read out from the photocell, and convert this reading to a percentage of illumination. To do so, we must know that the analog input of the Arduino returns a value going from 0 to 1,023 (10 bits). Therefore, we need to divide the reading from the input by 1,023. Then, to get a result in percent, we will multiply this value by 100:

```
float sensor_reading = analogRead(A0);
float light = sensor_reading/1024*100;
```

When the measurements are done, we print out the value of each of them on the serial port so that we can visualize the data. This is for example the code that prints out the temperature:

```
Serial.print("Temperature: ");
Serial.print((int)temperature);
Serial.println(" C");
```

We will also repeat each `loop()` function every 500 ms:

```
delay(500);
```

> Note that all the code for this chapter can be found inside the GitHub repository of the book at `https://github.com/marcoschwartz/arduino-android-blueprints`.

It's now time to test this simple Arduino sketch to check if our sensors are working. Upload the sketch to the Arduino board, and open the serial monitor (making sure the serial speed is set to 9,600). You should get a similar result inside the serial monitor, depending on your surroundings:

```
Temperature: 26 C
Humidity: 35%
Light: 75.42%
```

Writing the Arduino sketch

Now that we know that our sensors are working correctly, we can write the final sketch that allows the Arduino board to be accessed by the Android application we will write later on. The following is the complete sketch for this part:

```
// Control Arduino board from BLE

// Enable lightweight
#define LIGHTWEIGHT 1

// Libraries
#include <SPI.h>
#include "Adafruit_BLE_UART.h"
#include <aREST.h>
#include "DHT.h"

// Pins
#define ADAFRUITBLE_REQ 10
#define ADAFRUITBLE_RDY 2
#define ADAFRUITBLE_RST 9

// DHT sensor
#define DHTPIN 7
#define DHTTYPE DHT11

// DHT instance
DHT dht(DHTPIN, DHTTYPE);

// Create aREST instance
aREST rest = aREST();

// BLE instance
Adafruit_BLE_UART BTLEserial = Adafruit_BLE_UART(ADAFRUITBLE_REQ,
ADAFRUITBLE_RDY, ADAFRUITBLE_RST);
```

```
// Variables to be exposed to the API
int temperature;
int humidity;
int light;

void setup(void)
{
  // Start Serial
  Serial.begin(9600);

  // Start BLE
  BTLEserial.begin();

  // Give name and ID to device
  rest.set_id("001");
  rest.set_name("weather_station");

  // Expose variables to API
  rest.variable("temperature",&temperature);
  rest.variable("humidity",&humidity);
  rest.variable("light",&light);

   // Init DHT
  dht.begin();

  // Welcome message
  Serial.println("Weather station started");
}

void loop() {

  // Measure from DHT
  float t = dht.readTemperature();
  float h = dht.readHumidity();
  temperature = (int)t;
  humidity = (int)h;

  // Measure light level
  float sensor_reading = analogRead(A0);
  light = (int)(sensor_reading/1024*100);

  // Tell the nRF8001 to do whatever it should be working on.
  BTLEserial.pollACI();
```

```
    // Ask what is our current status
    aci_evt_opcode_t status = BTLEserial.getState();

    // Handle REST calls
    if (status == ACI_EVT_CONNECTED) {
      rest.handle(BTLEserial);
    }
  }
```

Now, let's look at this sketch in more detail. Some of the parts are similar to the sketch we saw earlier to test the sensor; we will not detail these parts again. It starts by declaring that we want to use the lightweight mode of the aREST library:

```
#define LIGHTWEIGHT 1
```

Then, we will define that we want to use the library for the Bluetooth chip, the aREST library, and the library for the DHT sensor:

```
#include <SPI.h>
#include "Adafruit_BLE_UART.h"
#include <aREST.h>
#include "DHT.h"
```

After this, we will define the pins on which we connected the BLE module:

```
#define ADAFRUITBLE_REQ 10
#define ADAFRUITBLE_RDY 2
#define ADAFRUITBLE_RST 9
```

We need to create an instance of the aREST library:

```
aREST rest = aREST();
```

We also need to create an instance of the BLE module:

```
Adafruit_BLE_UART BTLEserial = Adafruit_BLE_UART(ADAFRUITBLE_REQ,
ADAFRUITBLE_RDY, ADAFRUITBLE_RST);
```

Just before the `setup()` function of the sketch, we will declare the following three variables that contain the measurements coming from the sensor:

```
int temperature;
int humidity;
int light;
```

Then, in the `setup()` function of the sketch, we will initialize the BLE module:

```
BTLEserial.begin();
```

After that, we will set an ID and a name for our project:

```
rest.set_id("001");
rest.set_name("weather_station");
```

We also have to expose the different measurement variables to the aREST API so that they can be accessed by the Android app:

```
rest.variable("temperature",&temperature);
rest.variable("humidity",&humidity);
rest.variable("light",&light);
```

In the `loop()` function of the sketch, we will poll the status of the BLE module:

```
BTLEserial.pollACI();
```

We will also get the state of the module and store it in a variable:

```
aci_evt_opcode_t status = BTLEserial.getState();
```

If this status indicates that the Bluetooth module is connected to another device, we will process the incoming request with the aREST library:

```
if (status == ACI_EVT_CONNECTED) {
    rest.handle(BTLEserial);
}
```

> Note that all the code for this chapter can be found inside the GitHub repository of the book at `https://github.com/marcoschwartz/arduino-android-blueprints`.

It's now time to upload the sketch to your Arduino board. When this is done, you can move on to the development of the Android app to control the Arduino board via the BLE sketch.

Wireframing our Android application and modifying the layout files

We will start off our BLE weather station project by creating a new project in Android Studio with a blank activity.

We will target our project for a minimum SDK of 18 and a maximum SDK of 19.

We will first start off by drawing a paper prototype of how our application will work and the basic user flow, as shown in the following image. This will help us understand how the application will work as well as facilitating our development process.

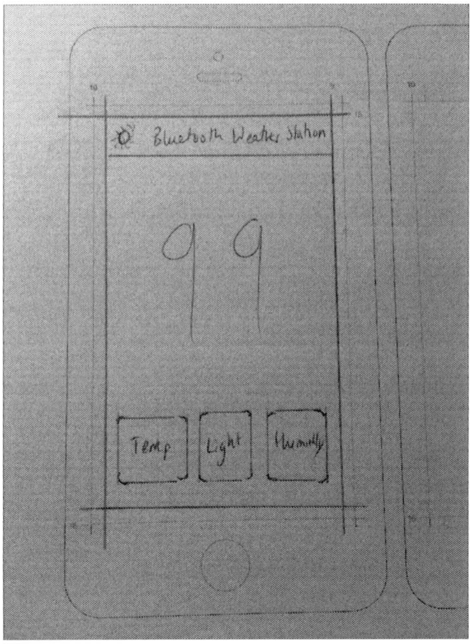

Upon analyzing the preceding image, we can see that this design will require two `TextView` objects. The upper `TextView` object will show all the Bluetooth callbacks, state changes, and characteristics written to the BLE module, while the lower `TextView` object will show the output from the temperature, light, and humidity sensor depending on which button was tapped.

The `TextView` objects will give them the following IDs:

- `connectionStatusView`
- `dataOutputTextView`

In the lower part of the layout, we will have three buttons reflecting the three parameters that we will be requesting, that is, temperature, light, and humidity. We will name the buttons as follows:

- The temperature button will be named as follows:
    - **Text**: `Temperature`
    - **ID**: `temperatureButton`

- The humidity button will be named as follows:
    - **Text**: `Humidity`
    - **ID**: `humidityButton`
- The light button will be named as follows:
    - **Text**: `Light`
    - **ID**: `lightButton`

Implementing Android layouts in the main activity

Before we embark on this project, we will enable the `Auto-Import` function, which will enable us to compile our project even more effectively and gives us one thing less to worry about.

You can enable `Auto-Import` by going to the **Preferences** option and selecting all the available options. The **Auto-Import** preferences are available on Mac and Windows as follows:

- On a Mac, navigate to **Android Studio** > **Preferences** > **Editor** > **Auto-Import**
- On Windows, navigate to **File** > **Settings** > **Editor** > **Auto-Import**

With all the necessary settings in place, we will first start off by creating a new project, where we will choose the following within the **New Project** setup:

- **Name**: `Bluetooth Weather Station`
- **Minimum SDK**: `18`
- **Project**: `Blank Activity`
- **Activity Name**: `MainActivity`
- **Domain**: `arduinoandroid.com`

We will build on our previous project in *Chapter 2, Controlling an Arduino Board via Bluetooth*, that is, the Arduino BLE Android project will start off by importing the `arduinoBLE` project from the Github repository and clone it to our desktop or download it as a ZIP file as explained in *Chapter 2, Controlling an Arduino Board via Bluetooth*.

Once imported, we will open `MainActivity.java`, select all the code below the `import` statement and copy it. When all the code has been copied, we will open our current project (Android Bluetooth Weather Station), go into `MainActivity.java`, delete all the code below the `import` statement, and paste the code.

In case you get stuck at this stage of the project, our code will be available in the repository in two stages, the version with all the necessary code that needs to be modified and the completed project. These are all available in the GitHub repository at `https://github.com/marcoschwartz/arduino-android-blueprints`.

Once the code is in our project, we will proceed by changing references to the UI elements to reflect our latest additions to the Android layout file in the `onCreate()` method:

```
dataOutput = (TextView) findViewById(R.id.dataOutputTextView);
connectionOutput = (TextView) findViewById(R.id.connectionStatusView);

adapter = BluetoothAdapter.getDefaultAdapter();
temperature = (Button) findViewById(R.id.temperatureButton);
light = (Button) findViewById(R.id.lightButton);
humidity = (Button) findViewById(R.id.humidityButton);
```

In this project, we will modify `onClickListeners` to connect to the buttons that we have included in the Android layout file:

```
temperature.setOnClickListener(new View.OnClickListener() {
            public void onClick(View v) {
                String setTempMessage = "/temperature /";
                tx.setValue(setTempMessage.getBytes(Charset.
forName("UTF-8")));
                if (gatt.writeCharacteristic(tx)) {
                    writeLine("Sent: " + setTempMessage);
                } else {
                    writeLine("Couldn't write TX characteristic!");
                }


            }
        });

        light.setOnClickListener(new View.OnClickListener() {
            public void onClick(View v) {
                String setLightMessage = "/light /";
                tx.setValue(setLightMessage.getBytes(Charset.
forName("UTF-8")));
                if (gatt.writeCharacteristic(tx)) {
```

```
                    writeLine("Sent: " + setLightMessage);
                }
                else {
                    writeLine("Couldn't write TX characteristic!");
                }
            }
        });

        humidity.setOnClickListener(new View.OnClickListener() {
            public void onClick(View v) {
                String setHumidityMessage = "/humidity /";
                tx.setValue(setHumidityMessage.getBytes(Charset.
forName("UTF-8")));
                if (gatt.writeCharacteristic(tx)) {
                    writeLine("Sent: " + setHumidityMessage);
                }
                else {
                    writeLine("Couldn't write TX characteristic!");
                }
            }
        });
```

We will also modify the code that deals with writing `remoteCharacteristics`, namely, the `writeLine()` method, and in addition, we will add another method known as `writeSensorData()`, which will deal with the remote data arriving from our different sensors:

```
private void writeLine(final CharSequence text) {
        runOnUiThread(new Runnable() {
            @Override
            public void run() {
                connectionOutput.setText("");
                connectionOutput.append(text);
                connectionOutput.append("\n");
            }
        });
    }

    //Implement the method below to output temperature/humidity/light
readings to dataOutputView

    private void writeSensorData(final CharSequence text) {
        runOnUiThread(new Runnable() {
            @Override
            public void run() {
```

```
                    Log.e(LOG_TAG,text.toString());
                    output=text.toString().trim();
                    if (output.length() > 0 && output.length() <=3) {

                        dataOutput.setText(output);
                    }
                    else {
                        return;
                    }
                }
            });
        }
```

Before we are able to move ahead with compiling the project, we need to work on the `onCharacteristicChanged` method so that the data that is received from the sensor data will be set to the `dataOutput` text view:

```
public void onCharacteristicChanged(BluetoothGatt gatt,
BluetoothGattCharacteristic characteristic) {
            super.onCharacteristicChanged(gatt, characteristic);
            writeSensorData(characteristic.getStringValue(0));
        }
```

At this point in time, the project will be unable to function as the necessary permissions have not been implemented yet. User permissions are necessary as it allows the application to access different capabilities of the device. In this case, we will need to add the following two permissions within the `AndroidManifest.xml` file, which you will find by navigating to `app` > `src` > `main` > `AndroidManifest.xml`:

```
<uses-permission android:name="android.permission.BLUETOOTH"/>
     <uses-permission android:name="android.permission.BLUETOOTH_
ADMIN"/>
```

When we perform all these changes, we should expect the rudimentary user interface to look as follows, with the sensor data showing up after tapping on the different parameters:

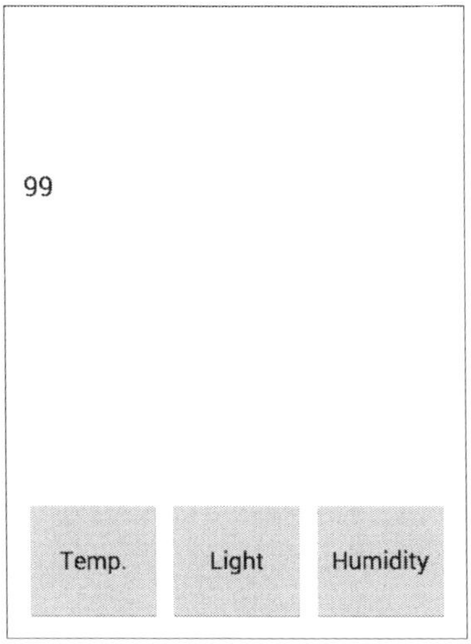

Enhancing the user interface

The current user interface requires further enhancements to make it user friendly. One can easily notice that the sensor data output needs to be enlarged and centered and the buttons can definitely be more attractive. Also, we want to make sure that our Weather Station app stands out from the user's current list of apps, so our app would definitely benefit from a change in the icon.

We will work on the following main tasks:

- Creating and adding our very own Android app icon
- Centering and enlarging the data output text
- Modifying the buttons and adding some color to our text

Creating and adding our very own app icon

One of our very first steps to enhance the user experience is to have our very own icon.

First, we will start off by downloading the image asset. This is available publicly at `http://bit.ly/chapter3-iclauncher`.

You should navigate using the project tree, followed by a right-click on app, as shown in the following screenshot:

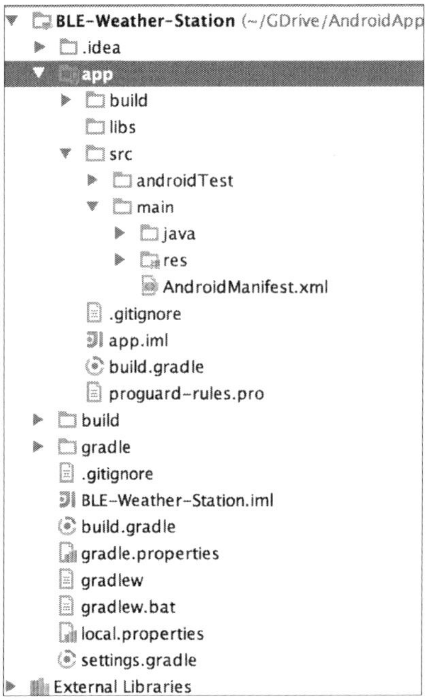

After you right-click on app, create a new image asset by going to **New** > **Image Asset**, as shown in the following screenshot:

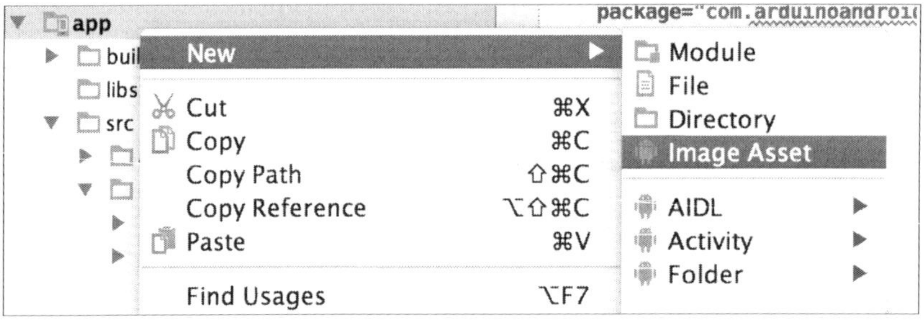

You will then be shown an **Asset Studio** pop-up window, which will allow you to choose your very own image file. For optimization purposes, we recommend going for a `.png` file with a resolution of 144 pixels by 144 pixels. Android Studio automatically does all the resizing and resource creation to adapt your graphic to different screens, as shown in the following screenshot:

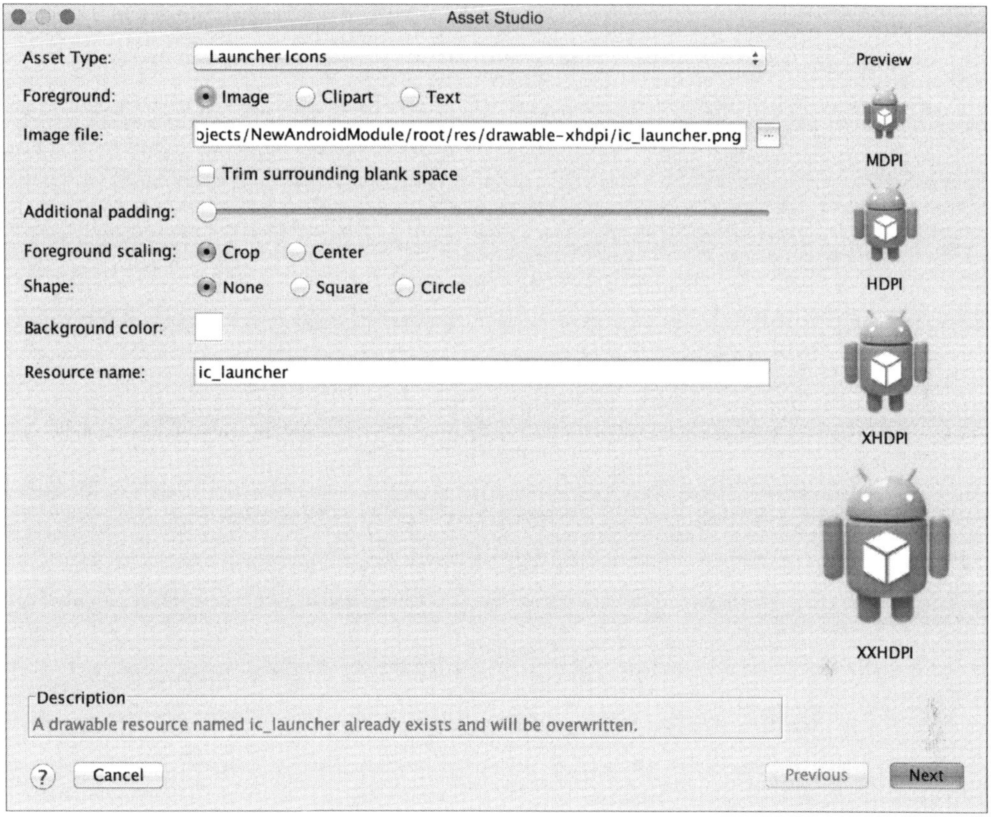

Once you choose the `ic_launcher` image file, which we have provided you with, you will be shown a screen with the icon in different sizes. Click on **Next**, where you will see the following screen:

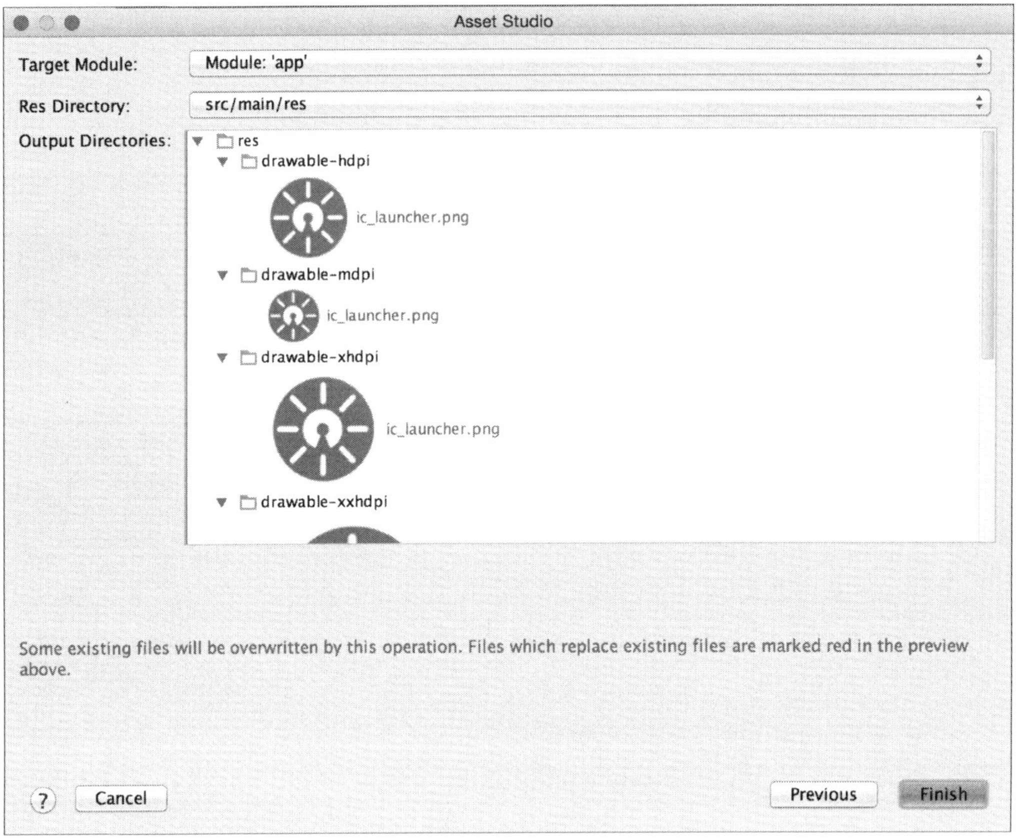

The preceding screen warns you that previous files will be overwritten and shows you the image launcher file in a number of different resolutions once again. Click on **Finish**, then compile the app, launch it on your physical device, and you should see something as pleasant as the following in your app tray and in the app's action bar:

Here's what the app's action bar will look like:

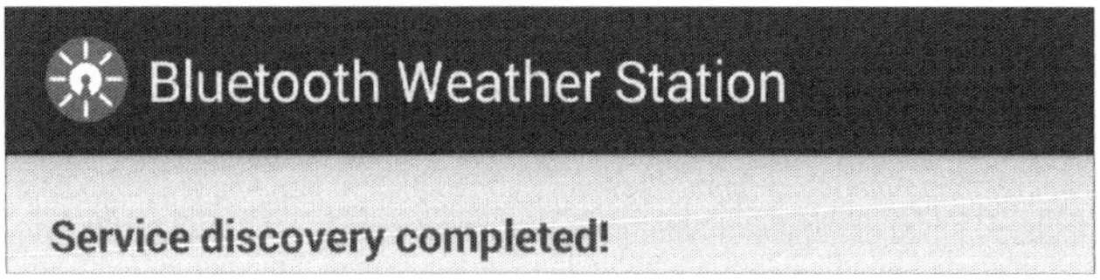

Centering and enlarging the data output text

In order to edit the layout for the main text output where the sensor data will be shown, we will need to open the project tree and navigate towards the layout file, which is available at `app` > `src` > `main` > `res` > `layout` > `activity_main_screen.xml`.

Once in this view, we recommend that you modify the text using the text view. This will allow you finer control and will also get you used to the different conventions used when editing Android layout files programmatically.

When opening the `activity_main_screen.xml` file, we will be seeing the different XML codes for the buttons and text views. At this point, look out for the code that takes care of the `Sensor Data Output` TextView and add the following code:

```
android:textSize="200dp"
    android:gravity="center"
```

The whole block of code responsible for the `Sensor Data Output` TextView will now look as follows:

```
<TextView
         android:layout_width="match_parent"
         android:layout_height="wrap_content"
android:textAppearance="?android:attr/textAppearanceLarge"
            android:id="@+id/dataOutputTextView"
            android:layout_gravity="center_vertical"
            android:textSize="200dp"
            android:gravity="center"
            android:text="99" />
```

In this block of code, we have temporarily used the placeholder text `99` so that we can approximate how it will look with the Android layout designer. With this modification, the sensor data output is now big enough to be seen by the user, thus enhancing the user experience.

Modifying the buttons and adding some color to our text

Finally, we will modify our buttons and add some color to the text by performing the following steps:

1. We will follow these two steps to create new buttons:
    1. Create a `drawable` folder with a new XML drawable file known as `buttonshape.xml`.
    2. We will then connect the drawable resource file to the main Android layout file.
2. Create the `drawable` folder by right-clicking on the `res` folder, which is available by navigating to `App` > `src` > `main` > `res`.
3. After creating the `drawable` folder within the `res` folder, we need to once again right-click on the new `drawable` folder and click on **New** and choose **Drawable resource file**, as shown in the following screenshot:

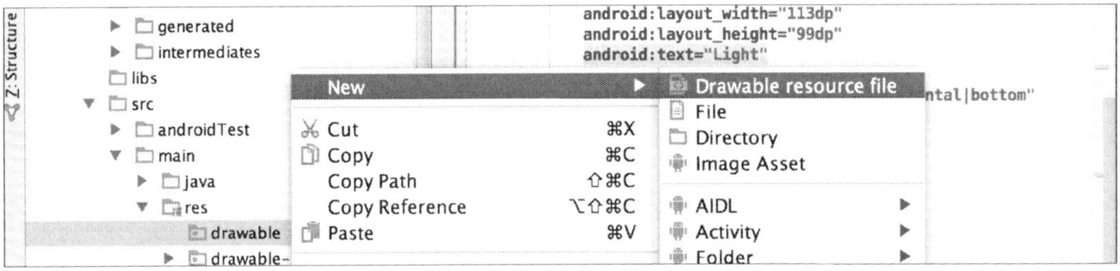

4. Name the file `buttonshape` and type down `shape` as the **Root element** followed by clicking on **OK**, as shown in the following screenshot:

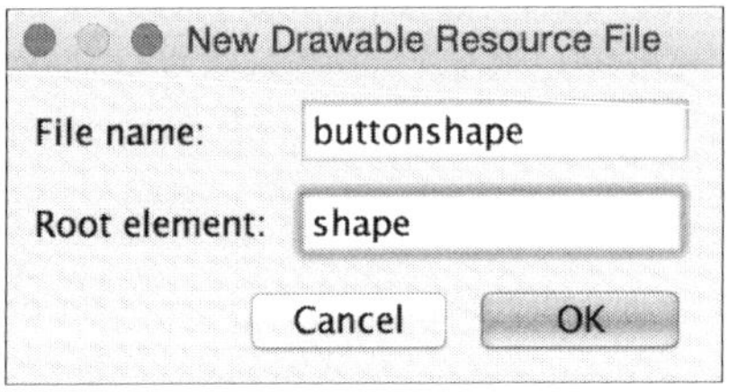

5. Within the `buttonshape.xml` file, we will add the following code:

```
<?xml version="1.0" encoding="utf-8"?>

<shape xmlns:android="http://schemas.android.com/apk/res/android">
    android:shape="rectangle" >
    <corners
        android:radius="10dp"
        />
    <solid
        android:color="#FFFFFF"
        />
    <padding
        android:left="0dp"
        android:top="0dp"
        android:right="0dp"
        android:bottom="0dp"
        />
    <size
        android:width="85dp"
        android:height="99dp"
        />
    <stroke
        android:width="2dp"
        android:color="#4A90E2"
        />
</shape>
```

6. Then, we go towards the `activity_main_screen.xml` file and refer to this drawable by including the following line of code within the button modules:

```
android:background="@drawable/buttonshape"
```

7. We will also add some flavor by adding the following line of code to the button and TextView modules within the `activity_main_screen.xml` file:

```
android:textColor="#4A90E2"
```

In the preceding code, `#4A90E2` refers to the hex code of the main color used in the app icon so that we maintain some consistency with the main user interface.

The final layout will look as follows on a Nexus 5 smartphone:

It's important to note that different Android devices have different dimensions. So, for your specific Android device, you might need to do further optimizations within the Android layout files to improve the interface.

How to go further

A large number of improvements could be done towards improving the user interface process within the Android app. Currently, service discovery is refreshed only by physically rotating the device, as the `onResume()` method is called upon rotation of the device. This could easily be improved by adding a refresh icon in the action bar and connecting this icon to the code, so that this method is called when the icon is tapped.

In addition, further user interface customizations can make it possible to personalize the app to your own liking; with regards to this app, you can get an idea of the possibilities by looking at the following links from the Android developers site:

- Button widget documentation at `http://developer.android.com/reference/android/widget/Button.html`
- TextView documentation at `http://developer.android.com/reference/android/widget/TextView.html`

You can even expand the app further with real-time monitoring, statistics, and trends.

Summary

In this chapter, we built a simple weather station using Arduino and Android. We attached several sensors to our Arduino board, along with a Bluetooth Low Energy module. We also built the corresponding Android app so that we can access all the data measured by the Arduino board just by tapping on a button of the phone.

In the next chapter, we will use a different technology to interact with an Arduino board via Android: Wi-Fi. We will build a smart power switch, to control an electrical device remotely, and also to measure the device power consumption via Wi-Fi.

4
Wi-Fi Smart Power Plug

In this chapter, we will build an open source version of a very commonly connected object—a Wi-Fi power plug. Indeed, these kind of plugs can be bought from many stores, and usually come with their own iOS or Android app.

In this chapter, we will build such a power plug from scratch, based on Arduino. We will connect a relay module, a current sensor, and a Wi-Fi module to an Arduino board to make our own Wi-Fi power plug. The power plug will be able to switch any device on and off, and will continuously measure the power consumption of the device.

We will build an Android app to switch on and off the power plug remotely via Wi-Fi. We will also be able to get the power output on request and display it on a screen.

The following topics will be the major takeaways from this chapter:

- Connecting a relay module, a current sensor, and a Wi-Fi module to Arduino
- Controlling the project by sending commands via Wi-Fi
- Building an Android application to control the project from a mobile phone or tablet

Hardware and software requirements

First, let's see the required hardware components for this chapter.

We need an Arduino Uno board. To control the lamp remotely (the lamp was used as an example in the chapter, but of course any 110V or 230V device can be used here), you will also need a relay module. We used a 5V relay module from Polulu, but you can use any 5V relay module that you want.

To measure the instant power consumption of the device connected to the plug, you will also need a current sensor. For this part, we will choose a breakout board based on the ACS712 chip. The following is a picture of the board I used:

You will also need a board that includes the CC3000 Wi-Fi chip, which we will use to receive commands via the Android device. For this project, we will choose a CC3000 breakout board from Adafruit. Of course, you can also use a shield from the same brand for this project; the code will be exactly the same.

To make the different connections, you will also need a breadboard and some jumper wires.

The following is a list of the components that were used in this project:

- The Arduino Uno board (`https://www.adafruit.com/products/50`)
- The 5V relay module (`http://www.pololu.com/product/2480`)
- The current sensor (`http://imall.iteadstudio.com/im120710011.html`)
- The Adafruit CC3000 Wi-Fi breakout board (`https://www.adafruit.com/product/1469`)
- The breadboard (`https://www.adafruit.com/products/64`)
- Jumper wires (`https://www.adafruit.com/products/1957`)

To connect a lamp or any other device to the project, you will need a pair of power cables: one male power plug and one female power plug. You will also need some screw terminals to make the required connections. The following is an image of the cables I used for this project:

Warning:

It can be dangerous to use high-voltage devices with such project. So, make sure to carefully follow all the instructions in the next section. Of course, you can make the entire project without connecting the project to the mains electricity; the principles are exactly the same.

On the software side, you will need the latest version of the Arduino IDE. You will need the library for the CC3000 chip found at `https://github.com/adafruit/Adafruit_CC3000_Library`.

You will also need the aREST library found at `https://github.com/marcoschwartz/aREST`.

To install an Arduino library, simply put the `library` folder into your `/libraries` folder inside your main `Arduino` folder.

Configuring the hardware

It's now time to assemble the hardware part of the project. Let's start by connecting the Adafruit CC3000 breakout board. First, connect the Arduino Uno +5V pin to the red rail on the breadboard, and the ground pin to the blue rail.

Then, connect the IRQ pin of the CC3000 board to pin number 3 of the Arduino board, **VBAT** to pin **5**, and **CS** to pin **10**. After that, you will need to connect the **SPI** pins to the Arduino board: **MOSI**, **MISO**, and **CLK** go to pins **11**, **12**, and **13**, respectively. Finally, take care of the power supply: **VIN** goes to the Arduino 5V (red power rail) and **GND** to **GND** (blue power rail).

The following is a schematic of the project, without the relay module connected:

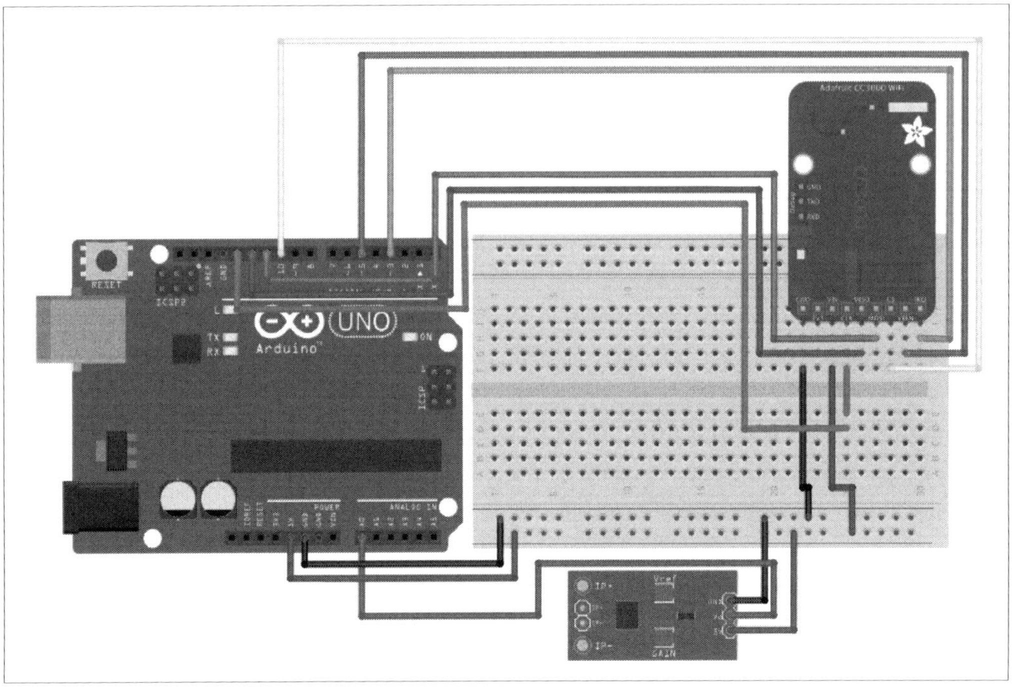

We will now connect the relay module. First, connect the power supply: the **VCC** pin of the relay goes to the red power rail, and the **GND** pin goes to the blue power rail. Then, connect the signal pin of the relay (usually denoted as SIG) to Arduino pin number **8** followed by the current sensor. Like the relay, connect the power first: the **VCC** pin of the relay goes to the red power rail, and the **GND** pin goes to the blue power rail. Then, connect the signal pin of the sensor (usually denoted as SIG or OUT) to Arduino analog pin **A0**.

We will now take care of connecting the project to the device you want to control, and to the mains electricity.

> Be very careful at this step as it involves high voltages (110V or 230V), which can be lethal. Also, make sure that you always connect the project to the mains electricity when you check everything else. When all other connections are done, make sure that you are not touching any bare cables. It is also recommended that you put the complete project in a plastic enclosure.

The following schematic describes how the different cables are connected to the relay and to the current sensor:

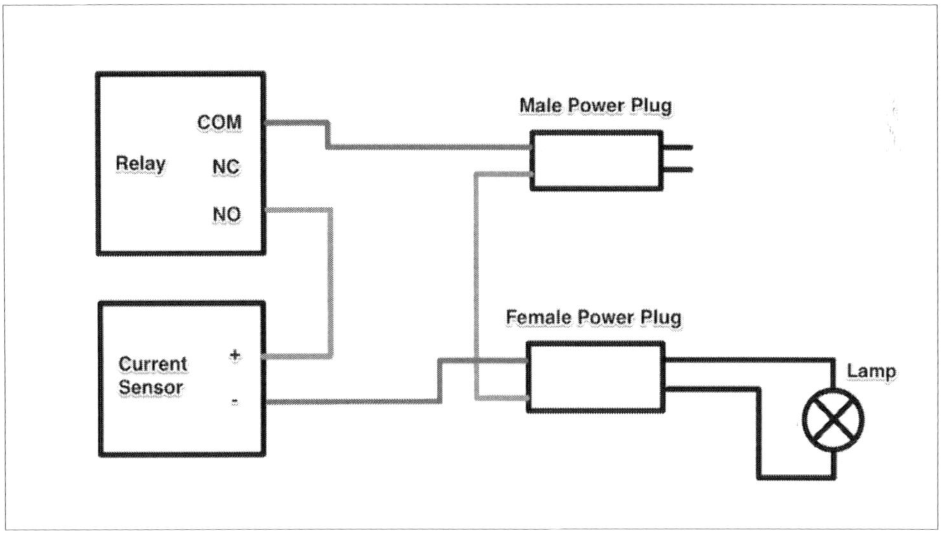

Note that as we are using AC voltages, the polarity of the cables doesn't matter here.

The following is an image illustrating the different connections between the cables, the relay, and the current sensor:

Finally, the following is an image of the complete project, with the male cable connected to the mains electricity, and a lamp connected to the female plug:

Testing the relay

We will now test the project, by testing the relay and switching it on and off. This will ensure that the relay is correctly connected to your Arduino board, and that the power cable connections are correctly done (otherwise, no electricity will flow through the connected device). Again, check every single connection before plugging the project into the mains electricity.

The following is the complete Arduino sketch for this part:

```
// Relay pin
const int relay_pin = 8;

void setup() {
  pinMode(relay_pin,OUTPUT);
}

void loop() {

  // Activate relay
  digitalWrite(relay_pin, HIGH);

  // Wait for 5 seconds
  delay(5000);

   // Deactivate relay
  digitalWrite(relay_pin, LOW);

  // Wait for 5 seconds
  delay(5000);
}
```

We will now consider the details of this sketch. It starts by declaring which pin the relay is connected to:

```
const int relay_pin = 8;
```

Then, in the `setup()` function of the sketch, we will declare this pin as an output:

```
pinMode(relay_pin,OUTPUT);
```

Finally, in the `loop()` function of the sketch, we will switch the pin from the on state to the off state every 5 seconds:

```
// Activate relay
digitalWrite(relay_pin, HIGH);

// Wait for 5 seconds
delay(5000);
```

Note that you can find the complete code for this part in the GitHub repository of the book at `https://github.com/marcoschwartz/arduino-android-blueprints`.

Make sure that everything is connected correctly, that you have a device (like a lamp) connected to our project and that the project is plugged into the mains electricity. Again, check that every connection is correctly made before plugging the project into the mains electricity. You can now upload the sketch to your Arduino board. You should hear the relay switching on and off, and see the lamp switching on and off as well.

Writing the Arduino sketch

Now that we are sure that the connections of the relay, the current sensor, and the power cables are correct, we will write an Arduino sketch to accept connections coming via Wi-Fi from the Android device.

The following is the complete sketch for this part:

```
// Import required libraries
#include <Adafruit_CC3000.h>
#include <SPI.h>
#include <aREST.h>

// Relay state
const int relay_pin = 8;

// Define measurement variables
float amplitude_current;
float effective_value;
float effective_voltage = 230.; // Set voltage to 230V (Europe) or
110V (US)
float zero_sensor;

// These are the pins for the CC3000 chip if you are using a breakout
board
#define ADAFRUIT_CC3000_IRQ   3
#define ADAFRUIT_CC3000_VBAT  5
#define ADAFRUIT_CC3000_CS    10

// Create CC3000 instance
Adafruit_CC3000 cc3000 = Adafruit_CC3000(ADAFRUIT_CC3000_CS, ADAFRUIT_
CC3000_IRQ, ADAFRUIT_CC3000_VBAT,
                                        SPI_CLOCK_DIV2);
```

```
// Create aREST instance
aREST rest = aREST();

// Your WiFi SSID and password
#define WLAN_SSID       "yourWiFiNetworkName"
#define WLAN_PASS       "yourPassword"
#define WLAN_SECURITY   WLAN_SEC_WPA2

// The port to listen for incoming TCP connections
#define LISTEN_PORT           80

// Server instance
Adafruit_CC3000_Server restServer(LISTEN_PORT);

// Variables to be exposed to the API
int power;

void setup(void)
{
  // Start Serial
  Serial.begin(115200);

  // Init variables and expose them to REST API
  rest.variable("power",&power);

  // Set relay pin to output
  pinMode(relay_pin,OUTPUT);

  // Calibrate sensor with null current
  zero_sensor = getSensorValue(A0);

  // Give name and ID to device
  rest.set_id("001");
  rest.set_name("smart_lamp");

  // Set up CC3000 and get connected to the wireless network.
  if (!cc3000.begin())
  {
    while(1);
  }

  if (!cc3000.connectToAP(WLAN_SSID, WLAN_PASS, WLAN_SECURITY)) {
    while(1);
  }
```

```
    while (!cc3000.checkDHCP())
    {
      delay(100);
    }

    // Display connection details
    displayConnectionDetails();

    // Start server
    restServer.begin();
    Serial.println(F("Listening for connections..."));
  }

  void loop() {

    // Perform power measurement
    float sensor_value = getSensorValue(A0);

    // Convert to current
    amplitude_current = (float)(sensor_value-zero_
  sensor)/1024*5/185*1000000;
    effective_value = amplitude_current/1.414;
    power = (int)(abs(effective_value*effective_voltage/1000));

    // Handle REST calls
    Adafruit_CC3000_ClientRef client = restServer.available();
    rest.handle(client);

  }

  // Function to display connection details
  bool displayConnectionDetails(void)
  {
    uint32_t ipAddress, netmask, gateway, dhcpserv, dnsserv;

    if(!cc3000.getIPAddress(&ipAddress, &netmask, &gateway, &dhcpserv,
  &dnsserv))
    {
      Serial.println(F("Unable to retrieve the IP Address!\r\n"));
      return false;
    }
    else
    {
```

```
      Serial.print(F("\nIP Addr: ")); cc3000.printIPdotsRev(ipAddress);
      Serial.print(F("\nNetmask: ")); cc3000.printIPdotsRev(netmask);
      Serial.print(F("\nGateway: ")); cc3000.printIPdotsRev(gateway);
      Serial.print(F("\nDHCPsrv: ")); cc3000.printIPdotsRev(dhcpserv);
      Serial.print(F("\nDNSserv: ")); cc3000.printIPdotsRev(dnsserv);
      Serial.println();
      return true;
    }
  }

  // Get the reading from the current sensor
  float getSensorValue(uint8_t pin)
  {
    uint16_t sensorValue;
    float avgSensor = 0;
    uint8_t nb_measurements = 100;
    for (uint8_t i = 0; i < nb_measurements; i++) {
      sensorValue = analogRead(pin);
      avgSensor = avgSensor + float(sensorValue);
    }
    avgSensor = avgSensor/float(nb_measurements);
    return avgSensor;
  }
```

Now, let's look in more detail at the Arduino sketch. It starts by importing the required libraries for this project:

```
#include <Adafruit_CC3000.h>
#include <SPI.h>
#include <CC3000_MDNS.h>
#include <aREST.h>
```

We also have to define which pin the relay module is connected to:

```
const int relay_pin = 8;
```

Then, we have to declare some variables that will help us to measure and calculate the power consumption of the device:

```
float amplitude_current;
float effective_value;
float effective_voltage = 230.; // Set voltage to 230V (Europe) or
110V (US)
float zero_sensor;
```

At this point, you should also change the value of the effective voltage so that it matches the voltage of your country.

Then, we have to define the pins on which the CC3000 Wi-Fi chip is connected to:

```
#define ADAFRUIT_CC3000_IRQ   3
#define ADAFRUIT_CC3000_VBAT  5
#define ADAFRUIT_CC3000_CS    10
```

We can now create an instance of the CC3000 Wi-Fi chip:

```
Adafruit_CC3000 cc3000 = Adafruit_CC3000(ADAFRUIT_CC3000_CS, ADAFRUIT_
CC3000_IRQ, ADAFRUIT_CC3000_VBAT,
                                         SPI_CLOCK_DIV2);
```

We will also need to create an instance of the aREST library:

```
aREST rest = aREST();
```

You will now have to modify the code to put your Wi-Fi network credentials:

```
#define WLAN_SSID       "yourWiFiNetworkName"
#define WLAN_PASS       "yourPassword"
#define WLAN_SECURITY   WLAN_SEC_WPA2
```

We will also define the port we want to listen to with the Wi-Fi chip:

```
#define LISTEN_PORT           80
```

After that, we will declare a server listening on that port:

```
Adafruit_CC3000_Server restServer(LISTEN_PORT);
```

Finally, we declare a variable that will contain the power consumption of the device, which will be accessible from the outside via HTTP requests (within the same local Wi-Fi network):

```
int power;
```

In the `setup()` function of the sketch, we will start the Serial connection:

```
Serial.begin(115200);
```

We will also expose the power consumption variable to the aREST API:

```
rest.variable("power",&power);
```

We will also declare the relay pin as an output:

```
pinMode(relay_pin,OUTPUT);
```

Then, we need to first take a measurement from the current sensor to get the value that the current sensor returns when no current is flowing through the connected device. This is done by a function that we won't detail here:

```
zero_sensor = getSensorValue(A0);
```

We will also assign an ID and name to our project:

```
rest.set_id("001");
rest.set_name("smart_lamp");
```

After this, we will call a function to display the details of the Wi-Fi connection, such as the CC3000 chip IP address:

```
displayConnectionDetails();
```

To end the `setup()` function, we will start our Wi-Fi server:

```
restServer.begin();
Serial.println(F("Listening for connections..."));
```

Now, in the `loop()` function of the sketch, we will read data from the sensor, which is connected on the analog pin A0:

```
float sensor_value = getSensorValue(A0);
```

Once we get this value, we can calculate the current from it as well as the device power consumption:

```
amplitude_current = (float)(sensor_value-zero_
sensor)/1024*5/185*1000000;
effective_value = amplitude_current/1.414;
power = (int)(abs(effective_value*effective_voltage/1000));
```

Basically, the manufacturer of the current sensor gives the first formula. Then, we get the effective current by dividing the amplitude current by the square root of 2, which is approximately 1.414. Finally, we get the effective power by multiplying the effective current with the effective voltage (and dividing it by 1,000 to have a result in Watts). Once the measurements are done, we process the incoming requests using the aREST library:

```
Adafruit_CC3000_ClientRef client = restServer.available();
rest.handle(client);
```

Note that you can find the complete code for this part inside the GitHub repository of the book at `https://github.com/marcoschwartz/arduino-android-blueprints`.

Don't forget to change the sketch to include your own Wi-Fi network name and Wi-Fi network password. You can now upload the code to your Arduino board, and open the Serial monitor. The following result is what you should see after a while (of course, the IP address of your board and the other parameters will probably be different):

```
IP Addr: 192.168.1.130
Netmask: 255.255.255.0
Gateway: 192.168.1.1
DHCPsrv: 0.0.0.0
DNSserv: 192.168.1.1
Listening for connections...
```

Write down the IP address that appeared in your Serial monitor—you will need it now, and while writing the Android application later. Now, we will test the Wi-Fi connection by sending some command to the project. You can go to your favorite web browser and type the following:

```
192.168.1.130/digital/8/1
```

Of course, you need to change the IP address with your own board's IP address as it was displayed in the Serial monitor. You should see that the relay instantly switches on, and you should be greeted by the following message:

```
{"message": "Pin D8 set to 1", "id": "001", "name": "smart_lamp",
"connected": true}
```

You can now switch it off again with:

```
192.168.1.130/digital/8/0
```

We are now going to try to read the power consumption of the device. You can do so by typing:

```
192.168.1.130/power
```

You should be greeted by the following answer:

```
{"power": 0, "id": "001", "name": "smart_lamp", "connected": true}
```

If you can see this, then it means that the sensor was correctly calibrated (as the power is 0) and that the power variable was correctly exposed to the aREST API.

Wireframing our Android application

The rigorous approach of wireframing our application before starting to write any code will help us provide a better user experience. The following is the paper prototype that we would like to follow when it comes to implementing our final code:

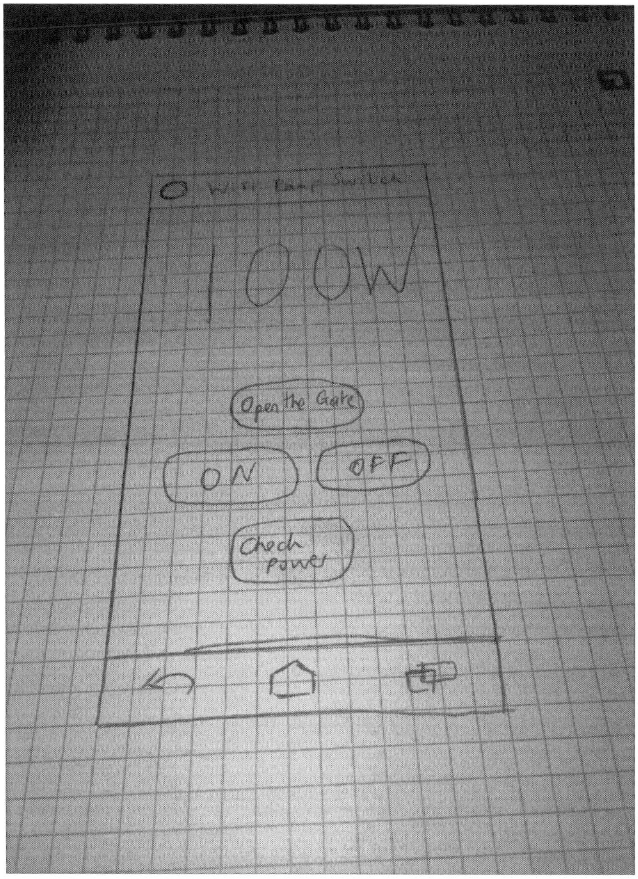

We will go ahead and create a new project entitled `Arduino Wifi` in Android Studio with a minimum SDK of 15 and maximum SDK of 19 (which at the time of writing is the most stable version of the Android SDK). This will enable us to cater to more than 80% of Android devices in the market. A project with a blank activity should be enough to start off this project.

Once you've got the project set up, we will go ahead and direct the Android layout files, which can be found by navigating to `app` > `src` > `res` > `layout` > `activity_main_screen.xml`.

We will apply a relative layout first, and within this layout, drag-and-drop four buttons together with a TextView, which will look roughly as follows (at this point, there is no need to focus on the aesthetic quality of the layout):

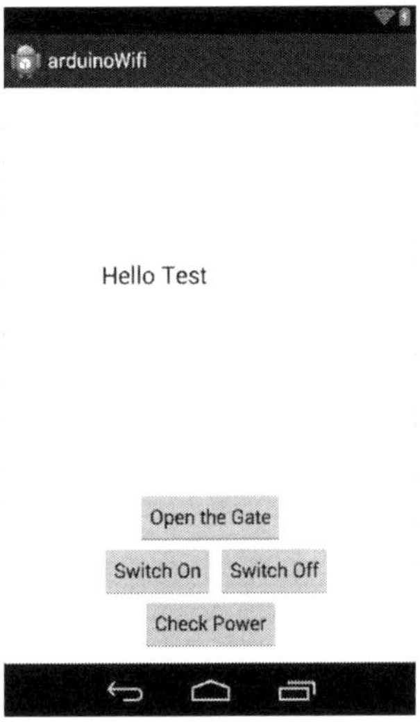

We will also identify each user interface item as follows:

- The **Open the Gate** button: `openGateButton`
- The **Switch On** button: `switchOnButton`
- The **Switch Off** button: `switchOffButton`
- The **Check Power** button: `checkPowerButton`
- The **Power Output** text view: `powerOutput`

Implementing our layouts into the code

We will first start off by declaring a `String TAG` object, which refers to `MainActivity` and which will be used for logging purposes:

```
public static final String TAG = MainScreen.class.getSimpleName();
```

Then, we will follow this by declaring all our view variables and assigning them to the `layout` elements within the `onCreate` method, which means that the `onCreate` method will look as follows:

```
@Override
    protected void onCreate(Bundle savedInstanceState) {
        super.onCreate(savedInstanceState);
```

```
        setContentView(R.layout.activity_main_screen);

        //Declare our View Variables and assign them to the layout
elements
        Button checkPowerButton = (Button) findViewById(R.
id.checkPowerButton);
        Button openTheGateButton = (Button) findViewById(R.
id.openGateButton);
        Button switchOnButton = (Button) findViewById(R.
id.switchOnButton);
        Button switchOffButton = (Button) findViewById(R.
id.switchOffButton);


        checkPowerButton.setOnClickListener(new View.OnClickListener()
{
            @Override
            public void onClick(View v) {
                if (isNetworkAvailable()) {
                    checkPowerTask getPowerTask = new
checkPowerTask();
                    getPowerTask.execute();
                }
            }
        });

        openTheGateButton.setOnClickListener(new View.
OnClickListener() {
            @Override
            public void onClick(View v) {
                if (isNetworkAvailable()) {
                    SwitchOpenTask switchOpenTask = new
SwitchOpenTask();
                    switchOpenTask.execute();
                }
            }
        });

        switchOnButton.setOnClickListener(new View.OnClickListener() {
            @Override
            public void onClick(View v) {
                if (isNetworkAvailable()) {
                    SwitchOnTask switchOnTask = new SwitchOnTask();
                    switchOnTask.execute();
                }
            }
```

```
        });

        switchOffButton.setOnClickListener(new View.OnClickListener()
{
            @Override
            public void onClick(View v) {
                if (isNetworkAvailable()) {
                    SwitchOffTask switchOffTask = new SwitchOffTask();
                    switchOffTask.execute();
                }
            }
        });

    }
```

As you can see in the preceding code, we refer to a number of ASync tasks, which we will refer to together with a JSON parser that we will be using to parse the data from the Arduino and adapt it to the power output text view.

ASync tasks will help us run the application tasks separately from the main user interface thread and hence significantly improve the responsiveness of the user interface and thus enhance the user experience.

With the following code, you will need to replace the `yourip` part with your own IP address, which you have found in the Arduino IDE Serial monitor. You will be able to declare the IP address within the `Main Activity` declaration as follows:

```
public static final String URL = "yourip";
```

We will then declare the following `AsyncTasks` object to enable the different actions we would like to achieve:

```
private class SwitchOpenTask extends AsyncTask<Object,Void,String> {

        @Override
        protected String doInBackground(Object... arg0) {

            int responseCode = -1;


            try {
                URL restApiUrl = new URL("http:// " + URL +
"mode/8/o");
                HttpURLConnection connection = (HttpURLConnection)
restApiUrl.openConnection();
                connection.connect();
```

```
                responseCode = connection.getResponseCode();
                Log.i(TAG, "Code" + responseCode);
            }
            catch(MalformedURLException e) {
                Log.e(TAG, "Malformed Exception Caught:", e);
            }
            catch(IOException e) {
                Log.e(TAG, "IO Exception Caught:", e);
                e.printStackTrace();
            }
            catch(Exception e){
                Log.e(TAG, "Generic Exception Caught:", e);
            }

            return "Code: " + responseCode;

        }

    }

    private class SwitchOnTask extends AsyncTask<Object,Void,String> {

        @Override
        protected String doInBackground(Object... arg0) {

            int responseCode = -1;

            try {
                URL restApiUrl = new URL("http://" + URL + "/
digital/8/1");
                HttpURLConnection connection = (HttpURLConnection)
restApiUrl.openConnection();
                connection.connect();

                responseCode = connection.getResponseCode();
                Log.i(TAG, "Code" + responseCode);
            }
            catch(MalformedURLException e) {
                Log.e(TAG, "Malformed Exception Caught:", e);
            }
            catch(IOException e) {
                Log.e(TAG, "IO Exception Caught:", e);
                e.printStackTrace();
            }
            catch(Exception e){
                Log.e(TAG, "Generic Exception Caught:", e);
            }
```

```
            return "Code: " + responseCode;

        }

    }

    private class SwitchOffTask extends AsyncTask<Object,Void,String>
{

        @Override
        protected String doInBackground(Object... arg0) {

            int responseCode = -1;

            try {
                URL restApiUrl = new URL("http://" + URL + "/
digital/8/0");
                HttpURLConnection connection = (HttpURLConnection)
restApiUrl.openConnection();
                connection.connect();

                responseCode = connection.getResponseCode();
                Log.i(TAG, "Code" + responseCode);
            }
            catch(MalformedURLException e) {
                Log.e(TAG, "Malformed Exception Caught:", e);
            }
            catch(IOException e) {
                Log.e(TAG, "IO Exception Caught:", e);
                e.printStackTrace();
            }
            catch(Exception e){
                Log.e(TAG, "Generic Exception Caught:", e);
            }

            return "Code: " + responseCode;

        }

    }

    private class checkPowerTask extends AsyncTask<Object,Void,String>
{

        @Override
        protected String doInBackground(Object... arg0) {

            int responseCode = -1;
            String result = null;
```

```
            try {
                URL restApiUrl = new URL("http://" + URL + "/power");
                HttpURLConnection connection = (HttpURLConnection)
restApiUrl.openConnection();
                connection.connect();
                responseCode = connection.getResponseCode();

                InputStream is = null;
                //http post request
                try{
                    String postQuery = "http://" + URL + "/power";
                    HttpClient httpclient = new DefaultHttpClient();
                    HttpPost httppost = new HttpPost(postQuery);
                    HttpResponse response = httpclient.
execute(httppost);
                    HttpEntity entity = response.getEntity();
                    is = entity.getContent();
                }catch(Exception e){
                    Log.e("log_tag", "Error in http connection "+e.
toString());
                }

                //convert response to string
                try{
                    BufferedReader reader = new BufferedReader(new Inp
utStreamReader(is,"UTF-8"),8);
                    StringBuilder sb = new StringBuilder();
                    String line = null;

                    while ((line = reader.readLine()) != null) {
                        sb.append(line + "\n");
                    }

                    is.close();

                    result=sb.toString();
                    Log.v(TAG,result);

                } catch(Exception e){
                    Log.e("log_tag", "Error converting result "+e.
toString());
                }

                //parse json data
                try {
```

```
                    JSONObject userObject = new JSONObject(result);
                    final String powerOutputText = userObject.
getString("power");

                    activity.runOnUiThread(new Runnable() {
                        @Override
                        public void run() {
                            TextView powerOutput = (TextView)
findViewById(R.id.powerOutput);
                            powerOutput.setText(powerOutputText +
"W");

                        }
                    });

                } catch(JSONException e){
                    Log.e(TAG, "JSON Exception Caught:", e);
                }
            }
            catch(MalformedURLException e) {
                Log.e(TAG, "Malformed Exception Caught:", e);
            }
            catch(IOException e) {
                Log.e(TAG, "IO Exception Caught:", e);
                e.printStackTrace();
            }
            catch(Exception e){
                Log.e(TAG, "Generic Exception Caught:", e);
            }

            return "Code: " + responseCode;
        }

    }
```

We will add another `helper` method at the bottom to make sure that Wi-Fi network connectivity is available:

```
private boolean isNetworkAvailable() {
        ConnectivityManager manager = (ConnectivityManager)
getSystemService(Context.CONNECTIVITY_SERVICE);
        NetworkInfo networkInfo = manager.getActiveNetworkInfo();

        boolean isAvailable = false;
        if (networkInfo != null && networkInfo.isConnected()) {
```

```
            isAvailable = true;
        }

        return isAvailable;

    }
```

Before going ahead, we will need to add the following permissions to our Android `Manifest` file, which is available at `app` > `src` > `main` > `AndroidManifest.xml`.

The following permissions will allow us to access the Wi-Fi network capabilities of the Android device:

```
    <uses-permission android:name="android.permission.INTERNET"/>
    <uses-permission android:name="android.permission.ACCESS_NETWORK_
STATE" />
    <uses-permission android:name="android.permission.ACCESS_WIFI_
STATE" />
```

After this, you can go ahead and compile the app. It's also important to note that Wi-Fi has a latency of about 300 ms and, depending on your Wi-Fi network, the value might take a significant amount of time to update the user interface.

If you are struggling with following along, you can also refer to the final project by checking out the GitHub repository at `https://github.com/marcoschwartz/arduino-android-blueprints`.

Polishing the user interface and experience

Once we have managed to finalize our code and assure ourselves that the user interface is being updated with the power value and that we can switch on and off the lamp, we can proceed to improve our user interface.

We will improve the user interface with the following main actions:

- Adding a new app icon
- Enlarging the power output text
- Aligning and styling the buttons
- Changing the application name in the action bar

Adding a new app icon

First, we will start off by downloading the image asset. It's available within the GitHub repository and as a public download at `http://bit.ly/iclauncherchapter4`.

You should navigate using the project tree, followed by a right-click on the `app` folder, as shown in the following screenshot:

When you right-click on `app`, create a new image asset by navigating to **New** > **Image Asset**, as shown in the following screenshot:

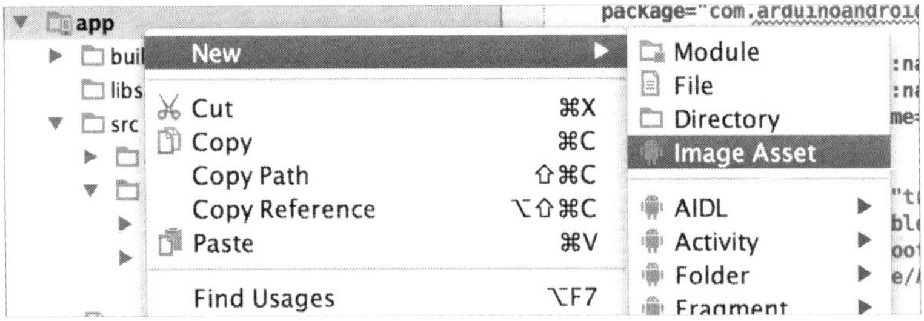

You will then be shown an **Asset Studio** pop-up window, which will allow you to choose your very own image file, as shown in the following screenshot. For optimization purposes, we recommend that you go for a `.png` file with a resolution of 144 pixels by 144 pixels. Android Studio automatically does all the resizing and resource creation to adapt your graphic to different screens:

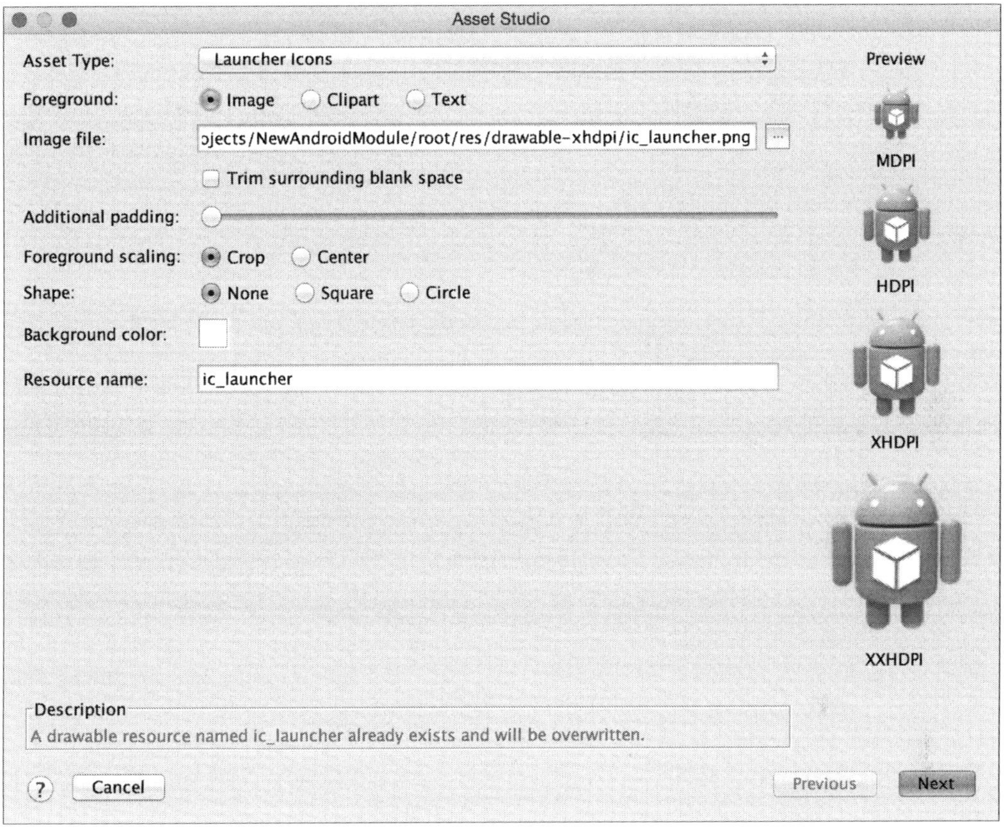

Once you choose the `ic_launcher` image file that we have provided you with, you will be shown a screen with the icon in different sizes. Click on **Next**, where you will see the following screen:

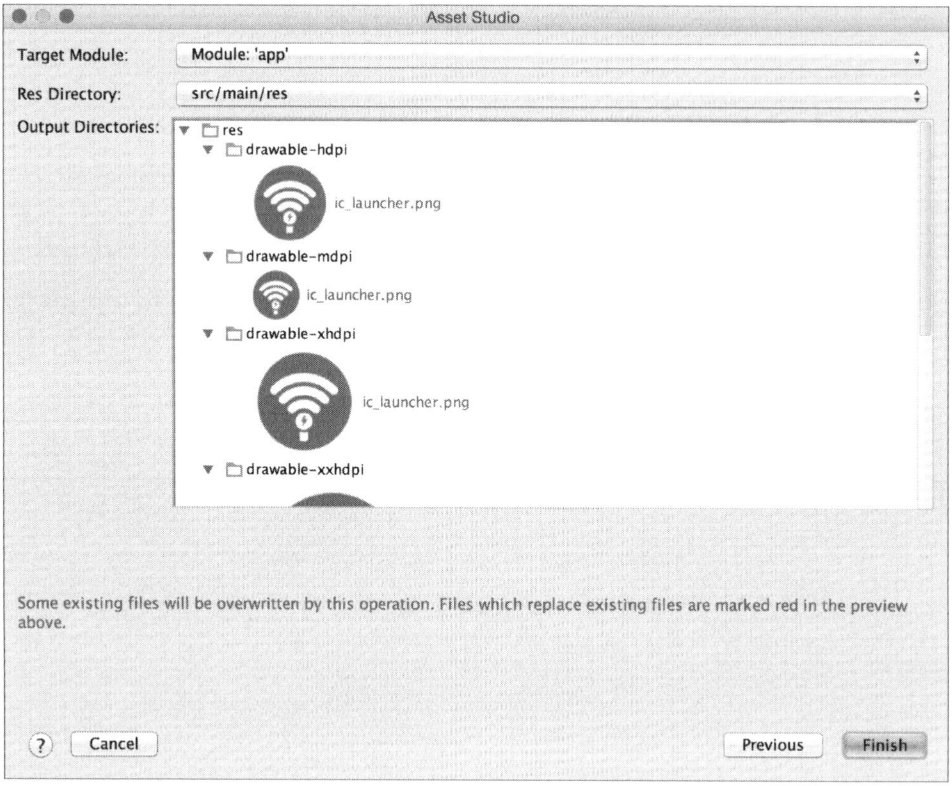

This screen warns you that the previous files will be overwritten and shows you the image launcher file in a number of different resolutions once again. Click on **Finish**, compile the app, launch it on your physical device, and you should see something pleasant in your app tray and in the app's action bar, which is shown as follows:

Centering and enlarging the data output text

In order to edit the layout for the main text output where the sensor data will be shown, we will need to open the project tree and navigate towards the layout file, which is available at `app` > `src` > `main` > `res` > `layout` > `activity_main_screen.xml`.

Once in this view, we recommend that you modify the text using the text view. This will allow you finer control and get you used to the different conventions used when editing Android layout files programmatically.

When opening the `activity_main_screen.xml` file, we will see the different XML codes for the buttons and Text Views. At this point, look out for the code that takes care of the `Power Data Output` TextView and add the following code:

```
android:textSize="100sp"
android:textAlignment="center"
```

The whole block of code responsible for the `Sensor Data Output` TextView will now look as follows:

```
<TextView
        android:layout_width="wrap_content"
        android:layout_height="wrap_content"
        android:text="100W"
        android:textSize="100sp"
        android:id="@+id/powerOutput"
        android:textAlignment="center"
        android:layout_alignParentTop="true"
        android:layout_centerHorizontal="true"
        android:layout_marginTop="78dp"
        />
```

In this block of code, we temporarily used the placeholder text `100W` so that we can approximate how it will look with the Android layout designer. With this modification, the sensor data is now big enough to show to the user and will be part of the enhancement within the user experience.

Aligning and styling the buttons

For our final steps, we will modify our buttons and add some color to the text.

There will be two steps when creating the new buttons:

1. Create a `drawable` folder with a new XML `drawable` file known as `button.xml`.
2. We will then connect the `drawable` resource file to the main Android layout file.

Create the `drawable` folder by right-clicking on the `res` folder, which is available at `app` > `src` > `main` > `res`.

After creating the `drawable` folder within the `res` folder, we need to once again right-click on the new `drawable` folder and navigate to **New** > **Drawable Resource File**.

Name the file `button` and type down `shape` as the root element followed by clicking on **OK**.

Within the `button.xml` file, we will add the following code:

```
<?xml version="1.0" encoding="utf-8"?>
<shape xmlns:android="http://schemas.android.com/apk/res/android">
    android:shape="rectangle" >
    <corners
        android:radius="30dp"/>
    <solid
        android:color="#FFFFFF"/>
    <padding
        android:left="0dp"
        android:top="0dp"
        android:right="0dp"
        android:bottom="0dp"/>
    <size
        android:width="120dp"
        android:height="60dp"/>
    <stroke
        android:width="2dp"
        android:color="#4A90E2"/>
</shape>
```

Then, we go towards the `activity_main_screen.xml` file and refer to this drawable by including the following line of code within the button modules:

```
android:background="@drawable/button"
```

We will add some flavor by adding the following line of code to the `Button` and `TextView` modules within the `activity_main_screen.xml` file:

```
android:textColor="#4A90E2"
```

The `#4A90E2` term refers to the hex code of the main color used in the app icon so that we maintain some consistency with the main user interface.

Changing the application name within the action bar

We all would like to customize the name of the app to one of our own liking and that will be the easiest thing within our project! We will just go over to the `strings.xml` file where we have all our constant text values within the project. This is available at `app` > `src` > `res` > `values` > `string.xml`.

Then, you can change the text of `arduinoWifi` to any name of your liking. In this case, we will stick to `WiFi Lamp Switch`:

```
<string name="app_name">WiFi Lamp Switch</string>
```

Our final project should now look as follows (device used in this case is a Nexus 4):

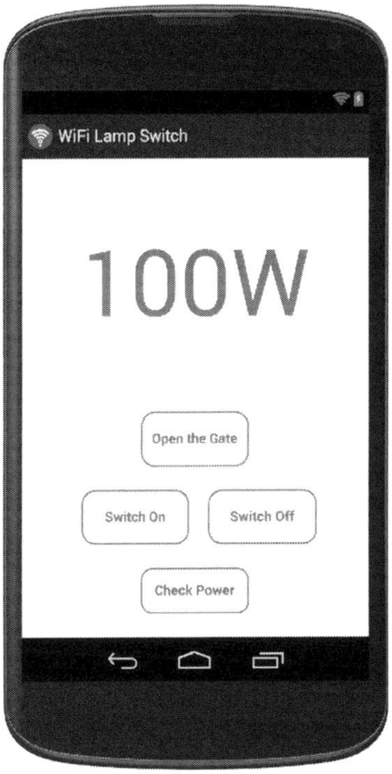

It's important to note that screen layouts might vary depending on different devices. In this case, you might have to adapt your Android layout file to your specific physical device.

How to go further

The options are endless when it comes to further modifying the Android app, and there are a number of implementations that can improve the app, such as real-time monitoring, where the power data output will refresh automatically. In addition, this data can provide a use case for data that is being generated to be stored in the cloud, which can be analyzed, allowing for the creation of graphical interpretations of this data. Such graphical interpretations can be correlated to the time of day and can help the user understand when the greatest power consumption occurs.

From a coding point of view, we can refactor our code, which implies that we simplify and reuse our code effectively. In fact, refactoring could definitely be achieved with the JSON parser, which could be refactored into its own class and which we opted on leaving out in the current setup so as to facilitate the learning process.

With regards to user experience, a new `EditText` field could be introduced together with a **Submit** button so as to allow the user to manually change the IP address, which will be called when discovering the IP address from the Arduino Serial monitor. Within this code, we use the concatenation and URL builder to form the right command.

Summary

We created a DIY version of a smart power switch, based on Arduino, and controlled by an Android application via Wi-Fi. We connected all the required components to the Arduino board, wrote an Arduino sketch to accept commands via Wi-Fi, and finally, created an Android application to control the switch remotely.

In the next chapter, we will use another Arduino board, called the Arduino Yún, where we will be able to plug an USB camera. As this board will have Wi-Fi as well, we will use the project to create a remote Wi-Fi security camera.

5
Wi-Fi Remote Security Camera

In this chapter, we will build a Wi-Fi remote security camera. The camera itself will be based on the Arduino Yùn and a standard USB webcam. The Arduino Yùn is a powerful Arduino board that has an onboard Linux machine and Wi-Fi connectivity. The Arduino Yùn will take the video coming from the camera and stream it on the local Wi-Fi network.

Then, we will be able to access the video stream from our physical Android device. This will give us the mobile flexibility to access our video stream from anywhere in our home.

From this chapter, you will learn how to:

- Use the Arduino Yùn and connect a USB camera to it
- Configure the Yùn to stream the video over your local Wi-Fi network
- Build an Android application to get the stream from the USB camera

Hardware and software requirements

The Wi-Fi remote security camera project is based around the Arduino Yùn board. The Arduino Yùn is a powerful Arduino board with integrated Wi-Fi and an onboard Linux machine based on a very small Linux distribution called OpenWrt. It also has a USB port so that you can connect hard drives, cameras, or other USB devices. We will use all these features in this project.

The following is an image of the board that was used in this project:

You will also need a USB camera to stream live video with the Yùn. You can basically get any camera that is compatible with **USB Video Class** (**UVC**). For this project, I used a Logitech C270 HD camera.

If you plan to use the camera for other applications, such as recording still pictures on the Yùn, you will also need a microSD card to save the data. Finally, you will need a micro USB cable to power the Yùn. The following is a list of all hardware components that are required for this chapter:

- Arduino Yùn (`https://www.adafruit.com/products/1498`)
- A UVC compatible USB camera (`http://en.wikipedia.org/wiki/List_of_USB_video_class_devices`)
- A micro USB cable
- A 4 GB microSD card, which is optional (`https://www.adafruit.com/products/102`)

You will need to configure your Arduino Yùn by following the official guide so that it can connect to your Wi-Fi network:

`http://arduino.cc/en/Guide/ArduinoYùn`

Note that you might have problems configuring your Arduino Yùn if you are behind a proxy. If this is the case, try disabling the proxy to see if it solves the problem.

If your Yùn is not recent, you might need to update OpenWrt (the Yùn's operating system) to the latest version. The procedure is described in the guide and can be found at `http://arduino.cc/en/Tutorial/YùnSysupgrade`.

After the Wi-Fi configuration is done, we will install the required packages to handle the camera and stream video on your local Wi-Fi network. Go to a terminal (use a terminal software, such as PuTTY or OpenSSH, if you are using Windows), and type the following command:

```
ssh root@yourYùnName.local
```

Of course, you need to change the command with the name of your Arduino Yùn that you defined when configuring it. If you forgot the name of your board, you will need to reset the Yùn and configure it again.

You will then be prompted to enter your password that you defined during the Yùn's configuration step. You will then be greeted by a screen similar to the one shown in the following screenshot:

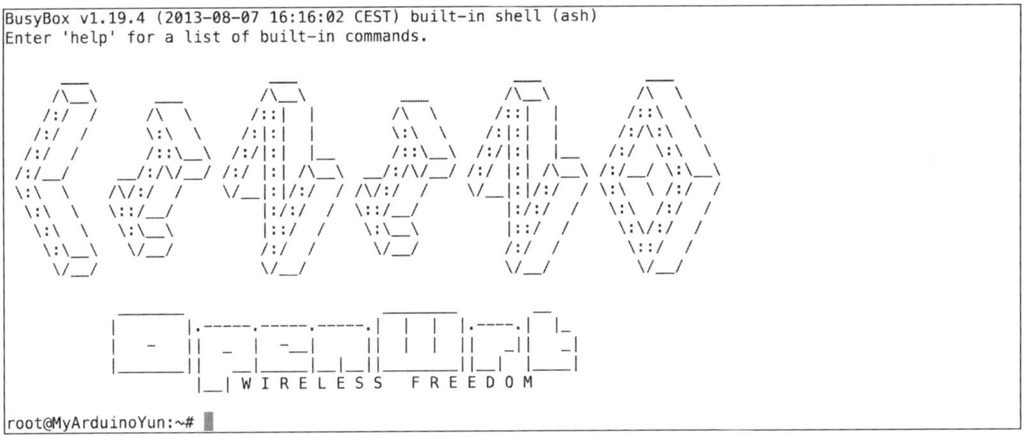

You can are now logged into the Arduino Yùn. You can type the following command to update the list of available packages:

```
opkg update
```

Then type this command to install the required packages for live video streaming:

```
opkg install kmod-video-uvc mjpg-streamer
```

Hardware configuration

The hardware configuration for this project is really simple. First, insert the formatted microSD card into the Arduino Yùn SD card reader, as shown in the following screenshot:

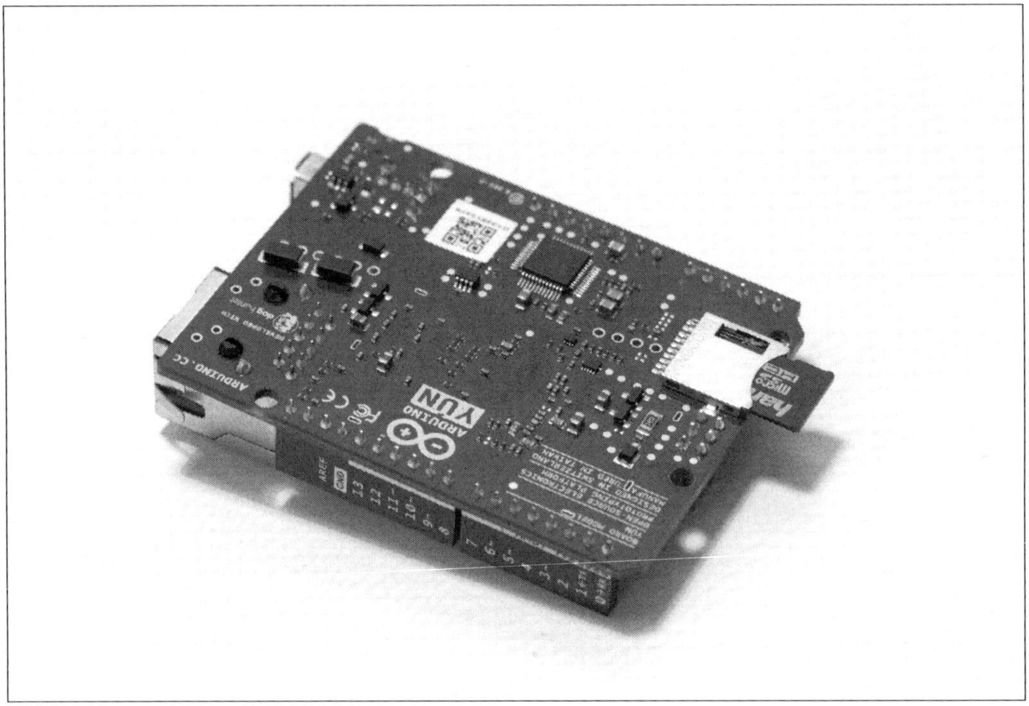

After this, you just have to connect the USB camera to the host USB port of the Yùn, as shown in the following screenshot:

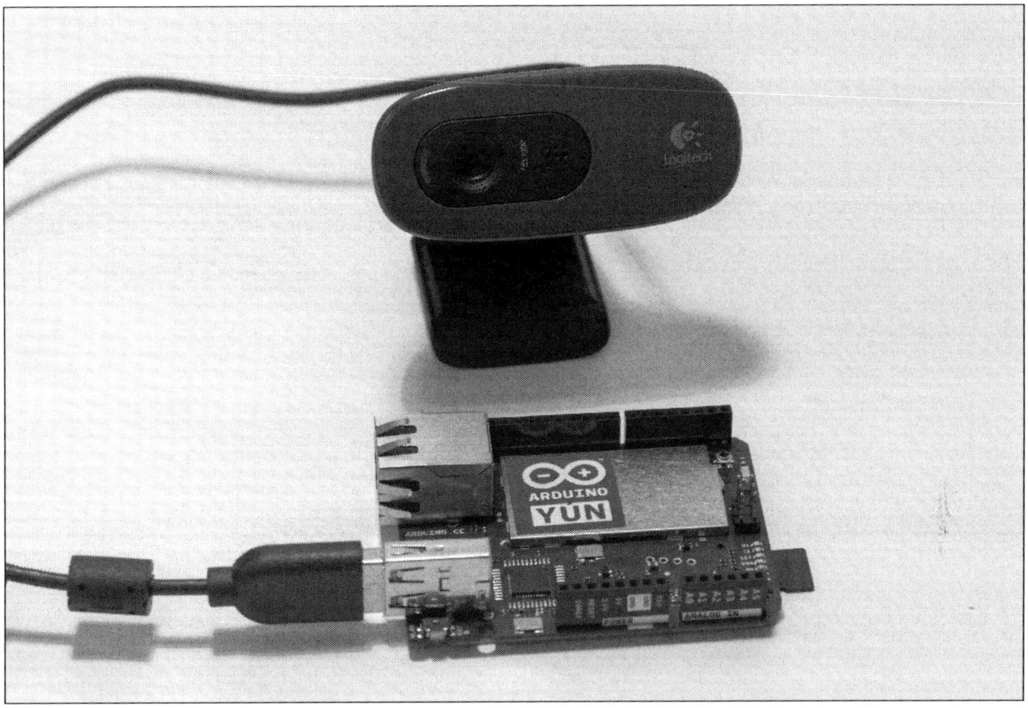

To finish the hardware configuration of the project, simply connect the board to power via the micro USB port (actually, you don't even need to connect it to your computer, the Arduino Yùn can work completely independently!).

Setting up video streaming

We will now set up the Arduino Yùn so that it continuously streams video. Once more log in to your Arduino Yùn using the following command:

```
ssh root@yourYùnName
```

Again, replace the command with the name of your Arduino Yùn. Then type the following command:

```
mjpg_streamer -i "input_uvc.so -d /dev/video0 -r 640x480 -f 25" -o
"output_http.so -p 8080 -w /www/webcam" &
```

This basically means that it will start the streaming at a resolution of 640 x 480, at 25 frames per second, and on the `8080` port.

You should see a series of commands being printed inside the terminal, meaning that the Yùn is now streaming live video on your Wi-Fi network. Now, go to your favorite web browser and type `yourYùnName.local:8080`.

This will open the main streaming interface, where you can select the desired streaming type. To access the stream itself for a test, go to `http://arduinoYùn.local:8080/stream.html`.

Note that this link is only valid within your own local Wi-Fi network. You will be greeted with the live stream coming from your Arduino Yùn, as shown in the following screenshot:

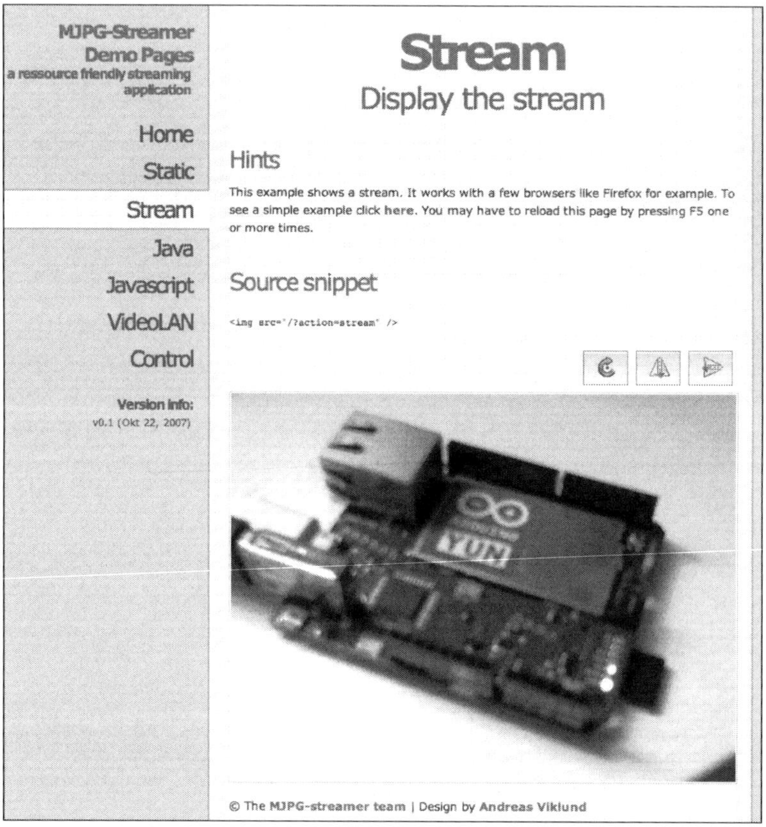

Implementing a fullscreen stream player on Android

In this project, we will implement a very simple Android app that will show the MJPEG stream from our Arduino Yùn. We will assume that you will have switched on the `Auto-Import` function within your Android Studio preferences. If not, kindly activate it by going to the **Auto-Import** preferences and selecting all the available options. The **Auto-Import** preferences are available on Mac and Windows as follows:

- **Mac**: **Android Studio** > **Preferences** > **Editor** > **Auto-Import**
- **Windows**: **File** > **Settings** > **Editor** > **Auto-Import**

With all the necessary settings in place, we will first start off by creating a new project where we will choose the following within the **New Project** setup:

- **Name**: `Android Yùn Security`
- **Minimum SDK**: `15`
- **Project**: `Blank Activity`
- **Activity Name**: `StreamActivity`

In this project, we will be working with three Java classes and we will need to create two classes, namely `MjpegInputStream` and `MjpegView`. The Java classes are as follows:

- `StreamActivity` (the main activity that is created upon the start of a new project)
- `MjpegInputStream`
- `MjpegView`

To create a new class, you will need to go to `app` > `src` > `main` > `java` > `com.domainofyourchoice.androidYùnsecurity`.

Right-click on the package name and go on **New** > **Java Class**, as shown in the following screenshot:

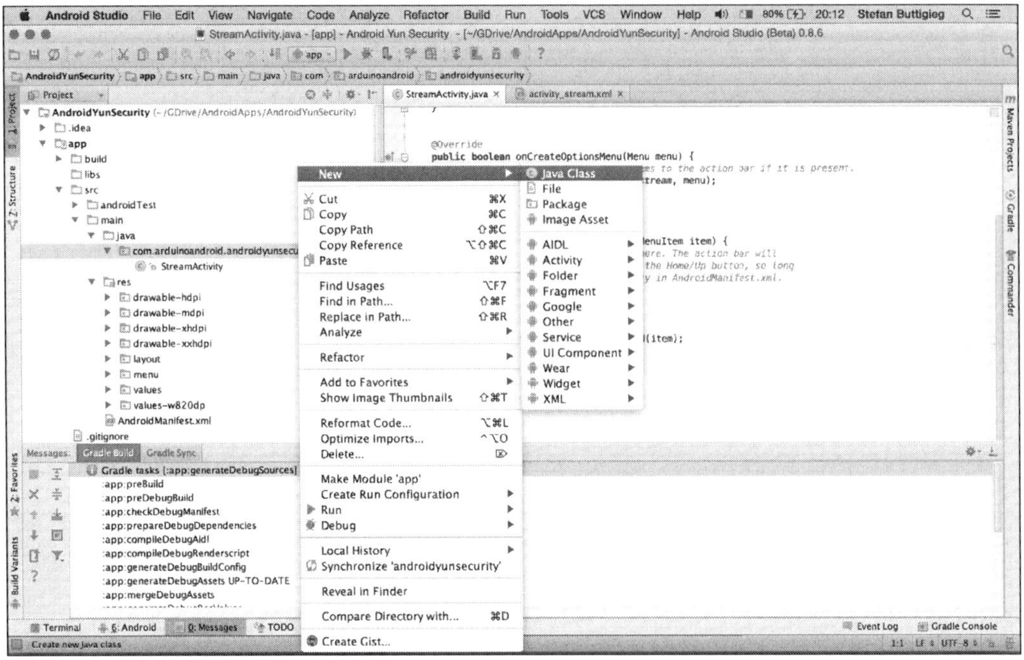

First things first; this application won't be able to work if we don't declare the Internet user permission. So, we head off to `AndroidManifest.xml` and we add the following line of code below the package name:

```
<uses-permission android:name="android.permission.INTERNET"/>
<uses-permission android:name="android.permission.ACCESS_WIFI_STATE"
```

The Android manifest will look as follows when completed:

```
<?xml version="1.0" encoding="utf-8"?>
<manifest xmlns:android="http://schemas.android.com/apk/res/android"
    package="com.arduinoandroid.androidYùnsecurity" >

    <uses-permission android:name="android.permission.ACCESS_WIFI_
STATE"/>
    <uses-permission android:name="android.permission.INTERNET"/>
```

```
    <application
        android:allowBackup="true"
        android:icon="@drawable/ic_launcher"
        android:label="@string/app_name"
        android:theme="@style/AppTheme" >
        <activity
            android:name=".StreamActivity"
            android:label="@string/app_name" >
            <intent-filter>
                <action android:name="android.intent.action.MAIN" />

                <category android:name="android.intent.category.
LAUNCHER" />
            </intent-filter>
        </activity>
    </application>

</manifest>
```

Then we head off to `StreamActivity.java` where we will start off our main streaming activity. In this project, we will use ASync tasks to do our network activity.

We will first declare `String TAG` (which we will be using for logging) and `MjpegView` (which refers to an instance of class that we have already created):

```
public class StreamActivity extends Activity {
    private static final String TAG = "MjpegActivity";

    private MjpegView mv;
```

In the `onCreate` method, we will declare our URL and also declare a number of parameters to set the video stream to fullscreen. It's important to replace `youripaddress` with the IP address that you can easily find out from the Arduino Yùn web panel:

```
    public void onCreate(Bundle savedInstanceState) {
        super.onCreate(savedInstanceState);

        //sample public ca
        String URL = "http://youripaddress:8080/?action=stream";

        requestWindowFeature(Window.FEATURE_NO_TITLE);
```

```
        getWindow().setFlags(WindowManager.LayoutParams.FLAG_
FULLSCREEN,
                WindowManager.LayoutParams.FLAG_FULLSCREEN);

        mv = new MjpegView(this);
        setContentView(mv);

        new DoRead().execute(URL);
    }
```

We will also need to declare the `onPause()` method that will be implemented when the Android application is closed, where this method will pause the live stream so as to not use the battery resources of the Android device:

```
    public void onPause() {
        super.onPause();
        mv.stopPlayback();
    }
```

After this, we will implement `DoRead AsyncTask`, which will perform `HttpRequest` and communicate with the Arduino Yùn server:

```
    public class DoRead extends AsyncTask<String, Void,
MjpegInputStream> {
        protected MjpegInputStream doInBackground(String... url) {

            HttpResponse res = null;
            DefaultHttpClient httpclient = new DefaultHttpClient();
            Log.d(TAG, "1. Sending http request");
            try {
                res = httpclient.execute(new HttpGet(URI.
create(url[0])));
                Log.d(TAG, "2. Request finished, status = " + res.
getStatusLine().getStatusCode());
                if(res.getStatusLine().getStatusCode()==401){
                    //You must turn off camera User Access Control
before this will work
                    return null;
                }
                return new MjpegInputStream(res.getEntity().
getContent());
            } catch (ClientProtocolException e) {
                e.printStackTrace();
                Log.d(TAG, "Request failed-ClientProtocolException",
e);
```

```
                //Error connecting to camera
            } catch (IOException e) {
                e.printStackTrace();
                Log.d(TAG, "Request failed-IOException", e);
                //Error connecting to camera
            }

            return null;
        }
```

Within the `StreamActivity.Java` class, we will implement `onPostExecute()`, which as part of the `AsyncTask` API will make sure that the video stream player shows up in the Main UI thread:

```
        protected void onPostExecute(MjpegInputStream result) {
            mv.setSource(result);
            mv.setDisplayMode(MjpegView.SIZE_BEST_FIT);
            mv.showFps(true);
        }
    }
}
```

We will then open `MjpegInputStream.java`, where we will declare all the necessary code needed to parse the data that is streamed from the Arduino Yùn to the Android device:

```
public class MjpegInputStream extends DataInputStream {
    private static final String TAG = "MjpegInputStream";

    private final byte[] SOI_MARKER = { (byte) 0xFF, (byte) 0xD8 };
    private final byte[] EOF_MARKER = { (byte) 0xFF, (byte) 0xD9 };
    private final String CONTENT_LENGTH = "Content-Length";
    private final static int HEADER_MAX_LENGTH = 100;
    private final static int FRAME_MAX_LENGTH = 40000 + HEADER_MAX_
LENGTH;
    private int mContentLength = -1;

    public MjpegInputStream(InputStream in) {
        super(new BufferedInputStream(in, FRAME_MAX_LENGTH));
    }

    private int getEndOfSeqeunce(DataInputStream in, byte[] sequence)
throws IOException {
```

```
        int seqIndex = 0;
        byte c;
        for(int i=0; i < FRAME_MAX_LENGTH; i++) {
            c = (byte) in.readUnsignedByte();
            if(c == sequence[seqIndex]) {
                seqIndex++;
                if(seqIndex == sequence.length) {
                    return i + 1;
                }
            } else {
                seqIndex = 0;
            }
        }
        return -1;
    }

    private int getStartOfSequence(DataInputStream in, byte[]
sequence) throws IOException {
        int end = getEndOfSeqeunce(in, sequence);
        return (end < 0) ? (-1) : (end - sequence.length);
    }

    private int parseContentLength(byte[] headerBytes) throws
IOException, NumberFormatException {
        ByteArrayInputStream headerIn = new ByteArrayInputStream(head
erBytes);
        Properties props = new Properties();
        props.load(headerIn);
        return Integer.parseInt(props.getProperty(CONTENT_LENGTH));
    }

    public Bitmap readMjpegFrame() throws IOException {
        mark(FRAME_MAX_LENGTH);
        int headerLen = getStartOfSequence(this, SOI_MARKER);
        reset();
        byte[] header = new byte[headerLen];
        readFully(header);
        try {
            mContentLength = parseContentLength(header);
        } catch (NumberFormatException nfe) {
            nfe.getStackTrace();
            Log.d(TAG, "catch NumberFormatException hit", nfe);
            mContentLength = getEndOfSeqeunce(this, EOF_MARKER);
        }
```

```
            reset();
            byte[] frameData = new byte[mContentLength];
            skipBytes(headerLen);
            readFully(frameData);
            return BitmapFactory.decodeStream(new ByteArrayInputStream(fr
ameData));
        }
    }
```

Last but not least, we will head off to `MjpegView.java`, where we will be declaring a number of important methods to consolidate all of our application processes. The `MjpegView.java` class is available at `http://git.io/_Mu_Gw`.

Replace all the code within your version of the `MjpegView.java` class with the one from the online repository and ensure that the package name and other class references match the ones within your project.

Once you make sure that all your `import` statements are included within each class with the `Auto-Import` function, you could go ahead and build the app and test it on your physical device that is connected to the same Wi-Fi Network as your Arduino Yùn.

The final project should look something as follows:

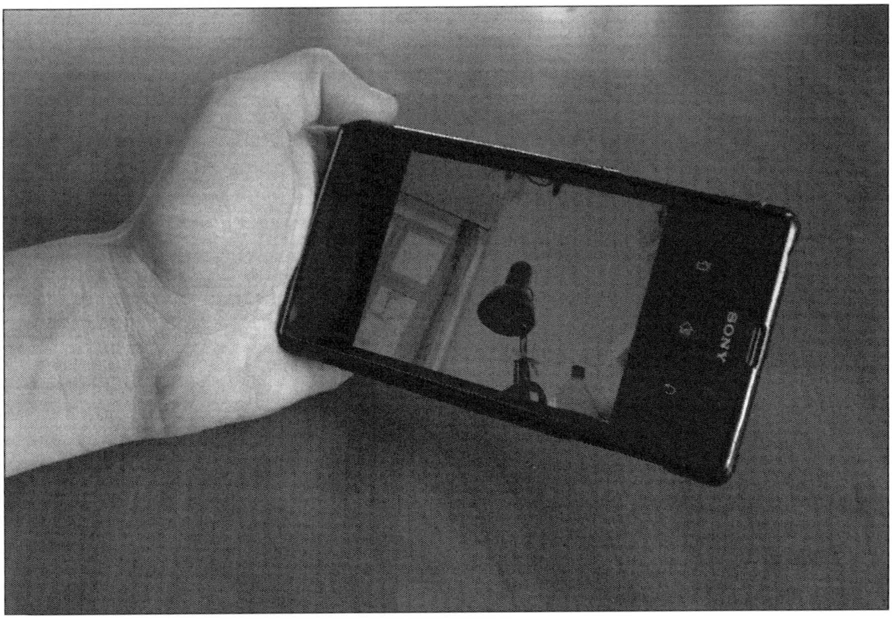

How to go further

An interesting implementation and further improvement on the basic Android app would be to include the ability to take a snapshot when motion is detected in front of the camera. This can be achieved through the OpenCV library for Android, which is available at `http://opencv.org/platforms/android.html`.

Furthermore, the user interface could be improved to include the ability to take a picture of that particular scene. This project could also be combined with the mobile robot project, which we shall talk about later on, to have a live-streaming mobile robot that can be controlled from the same Android application. The use cases for modifying such a setup are endless, starting from remote baby monitors to medical monitoring devices.

Summary

Let's summarize what we did in this chapter. We learned how to connect a USB camera to the Arduino Yùn, and configure the Arduino board so that it streams video to our local Wi-Fi network. Then we created a new Android application to watch the video stream of the camera on our Android phone or tablet. Therefore, we created a simple Wi-Fi security camera based on Arduino and Android.

In the next chapter, we will do something different. We will use the gyroscope of the Android phone to control a servomotor connected to an Arduino board. We will be able to control the angle of rotation of the servomotor just by titling the Android phone.

6
Android Phone Sensor

In this book so far, we have used an Android device to control Arduino projects and get readings from sensors connected to the Arduino board. In this chapter, we will do something different: we will use the phone's sensors to control an Arduino board.

We will connect a servomotor to an Arduino board so that it can be controlled from the Android phone. A servomotor is basically a motor whose angular position can be precisely controlled by a microcontroller. We will use BLE once more to receive commands from the Android device.

On the Android side, we will basically measure data coming from the phone's gyroscope sensor continuously and convert this data into meaningful commands for the servo. The goal is that the servo motor continuously follows the movement of the Android device.

In this chapter, you will learn how to:

- Connect a servo motor to the Arduino platform
- Write a sketch to receive commands via BLE
- Write an Android application to control the servomotor using the Android phone gyroscope

Hardware and software requirements

The first thing you will need for this project is an Arduino Uno board.

Then you will need a BLE module. We chose the Adafruit nRF8001 chip because it comes with a nice Arduino library, and it has already existing examples of Android apps to control the module.

For the servomotor, we chose a simple 5V servo motor module. You can use one from any brand you want, as long as it can be controlled with 5V voltage levels. The following is an image of the servo that was used for this project:

Finally, you will need a breadboard and some jumper wires to make the different connections.

This is the list of the required components for the project:

- Arduino Uno (`https://www.adafruit.com/product/50`)
- The Adafruit nRF8001 BLE breakout board (`https://www.adafruit.com/product/1697`)
- A 5V servo motor (`https://www.adafruit.com/product/1143`)
- The breadboard (`https://www.adafruit.com/products/64`)
- Jumper wires (`https://www.adafruit.com/products/1957`)

On the software side, you will need the usual Arduino IDE. It is recommended that you use the Arduino IDE Version 1.5.7 for this chapter.

You will need the following libraries:

- The library for the nRF8001 board found at `https://github.com/adafruit/Adafruit_nRF8001`
- The aREST library found at `https://github.com/marcoschwartz/aREST`

To install a given library, simply extract the `library` folder into your `Arduino/libraries` folder.

Configuring the hardware

Let's now make the necessary hardware connections for the project. To help you out, this is the schematic of the project:

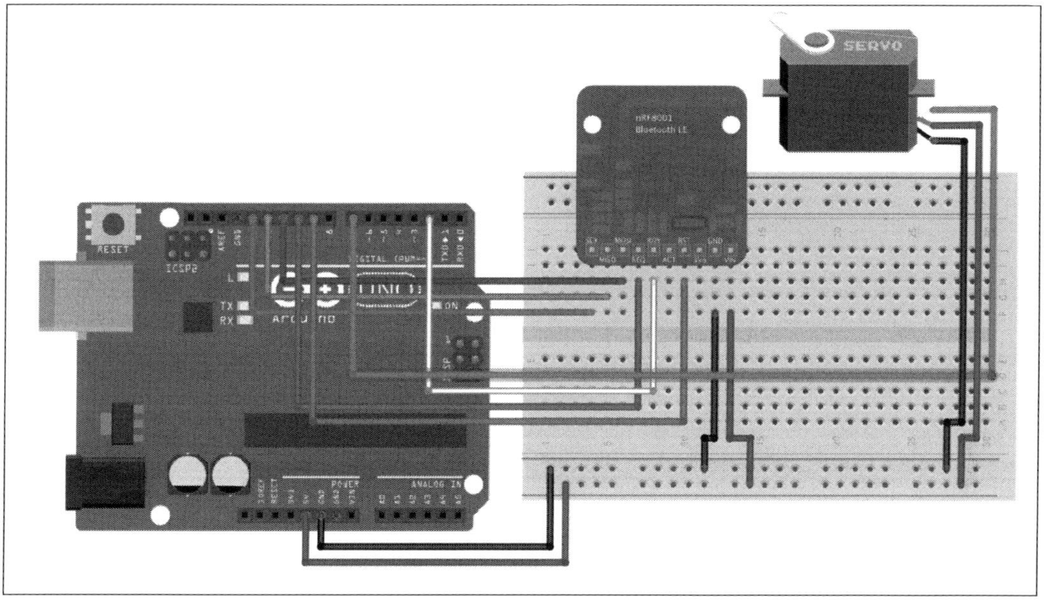

The first step is to place the Bluetooth module on the breadboard. Then, connect the power supply from the Arduino board to the breadboard: 5V of the Arduino board goes to the red power rail, and **GND** goes to the blue power rail.

We will connect the BLE module. First, connect the power supply of the module: GND goes to the blue power rail, and **VIN** goes to the red power rail. After this, you will need to connect the different wires responsible for the SPI interface: **SCK** to Arduino pin **13**, **MISO** to Arduino pin **12**, and **MOSI** to Arduino pin **11**. Then connect the **REQ** pin to Arduino pin **10**. Finally, connect the **RDY** pin to Arduino pin **2**, and the **RST** pin to Arduino pin **9**. If you need additional help to connect this module, you can visit the manufacturer's guide at `https://learn.adafruit.com/getting-started-with-the-nrf8001-bluefruit-le-breakout`.

For the servo motor, connect the red cable of the servo to the red power rail and the black cable of the servo to the blue power rail. Finally, connect the remaining cable to pin number 7 of the Arduino board.

The following is a picture of the assembled project:

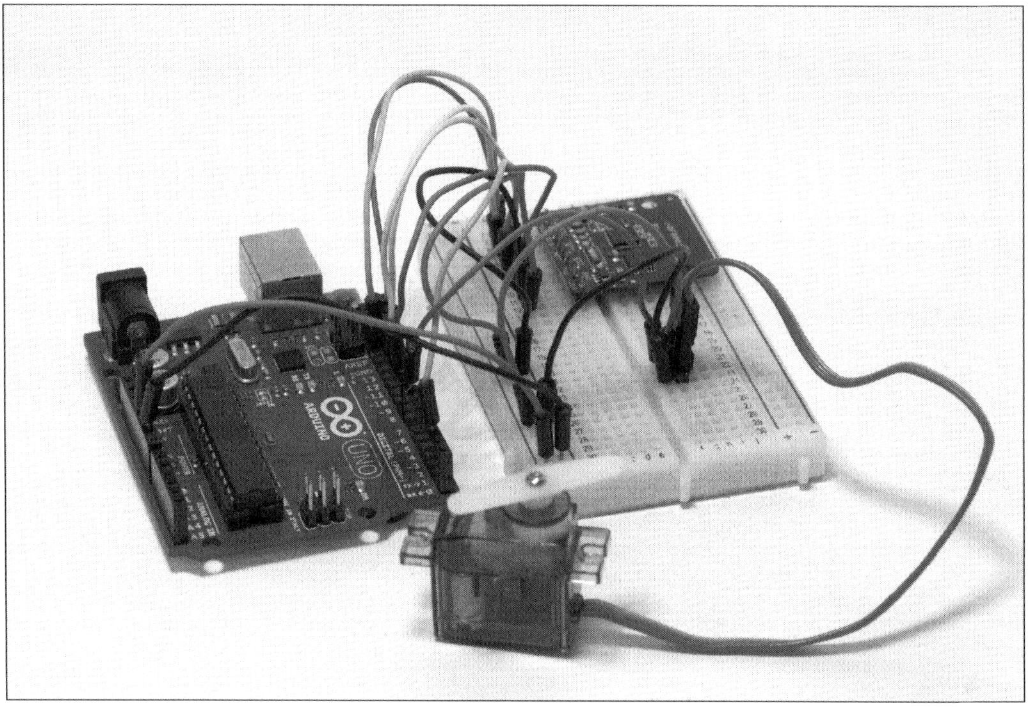

Testing the servo

We will now write a very simple sketch to test the servomotor and also see how the Arduino Servo library is working. The following is the complete sketch for this part:

```
#include <Servo.h>

// Create servo object
Servo myservo;

// Servo position
int pos = 0;

void setup()
{
  // Attaches the servo on pin 7 to the servo object
  myservo.attach(7);
```

```
}

void loop()
{
  // Goes from 0 degrees to 180 degrees
  for(pos = 0; pos < 180; pos += 1)
  {
    myservo.write(pos);
    delay(15);
  }

  // Goes from 180 degrees to 0 degrees
  for(pos = 180; pos >= 1; pos -= 1)
  {
    myservo.write(pos);
    delay(15);
  }
}
```

Let's now see the details of the sketch. This starts by including the Servo library as follows:

```
#include <Servo.h>
```

Then we create an instance of the Servo library:

```
Servo myservo;
```

We will also declare a variable called `pos` that will contain the angular position of the servo motor:

```
int pos = 0;
```

After this, in the `setup()` function of the sketch, we will attach the servo to pin 7 of the Arduino board:

```
myservo.attach(7);
```

After this, we will sweep the `pos` variable from `0` to `180`, meaning we cover all the possible angular positions of the servo motor:

```
for(pos = 0; pos < 180; pos += 1)
{
  myservo.write(pos);
  delay(15);
}
```

Still in this test code, we will make the servo motor go in the other direction with a similar loop.

> Note that all the code for this chapter can be found in the GitHub repository of the book at `https://github.com/marcoschwartz/arduino-android-blueprints`.

It's now time to test this Arduino sketch. Simply upload the code to the Arduino board. You should see that the servo motor is going all the way in one direction, and then going back to its starting position. After this, this loop should repeat itself. If this is working, you can move on to the next section.

Writing the Arduino sketch

We will now write the sketch to control the servo motor via BLE. This is the complete sketch for this part:

```
#include <SPI.h>
#include "Adafruit_BLE_UART.h"
#include <aREST.h>
#include <Servo.h>

// Lightweight mode
#define LIGHTWEIGHT 1

// Pins
#define ADAFRUITBLE_REQ 10
#define ADAFRUITBLE_RDY 2     // This should be pin 2 or 3
#define ADAFRUITBLE_RST 9

// Create servo object
Servo myservo;

// Create aREST instance
aREST rest = aREST();

// Servo position
int pos = 0;

// BLE instance
```

```
Adafruit_BLE_UART BTLEserial = Adafruit_BLE_UART(ADAFRUITBLE_REQ,
ADAFRUITBLE_RDY, ADAFRUITBLE_RST);

void setup()
{
   // Start Serial
  Serial.begin(115200);

  // Attaches the servo on pin 7 to the servo object
  myservo.attach(7);

  // Start BLE
  BTLEserial.begin();

  // Give name and ID to device
  rest.set_id("001");
  rest.set_name("servo_control");

  // Expose function to API
  rest.function("servo",servoControl);
}


void loop()
{
  // Tell the nRF8001 to do whatever it should be working on.
  BTLEserial.pollACI();

  // Ask what is our current status
  aci_evt_opcode_t status = BTLEserial.getState();

  // Handle REST calls
  if (status == ACI_EVT_CONNECTED) {
    rest.handle(BTLEserial);
  }
}

// Control servo from REST API
int servoControl(String command) {

  // Get position from command
  int pos = command.toInt();
```

```
    Serial.println(pos);

    myservo.write(pos);

    return 1;
  }
```

Let's now see the details of this sketch. It starts by including the required libraries for the project:

```
#include <SPI.h>
#include "Adafruit_BLE_UART.h"
#include <aREST.h>
#include <Servo.h>
```

We will also declare that we want to use the lightweight mode of the aREST library:

```
#define LIGHTWEIGHT 1
```

After this, we will define which pin the Bluetooth module is connected to:

```
#define ADAFRUITBLE_REQ 10
#define ADAFRUITBLE_RDY 2     // This should be an interrupt pin, on
Uno thats #2 or #3
#define ADAFRUITBLE_RST 9
```

We will also create an instance of the Servo library:

```
Servo myservo;
```

We will also need to create an instance of the aREST library:

```
aREST rest = aREST();
```

We will also need to create an instance of the nRF8001 library:

```
Adafruit_BLE_UART BTLEserial = Adafruit_BLE_UART(ADAFRUITBLE_REQ,
ADAFRUITBLE_RDY, ADAFRUITBLE_RST);
```

In the `setup()` function of the sketch, we will attach the servo motor to pin number 7 of the Arduino board:

```
myservo.attach(7);
```

We will also initialize the BLE board:

```
BTLEserial.begin();
```

After this, we will give a name and an ID to the board:

```
rest.set_id("001");
rest.set_name("servo_control");
```

We will also expose the `servoControl` function to the aREST API so that we can access it via Bluetooth. We will see the details of the `servoControl` function in a moment:

```
rest.function("servo",servoControl);
```

In the `loop()` function of the sketch, we will poll the Bluetooth chip to see if a device is connected to it:

```
BTLEserial.pollACI();
```

We will store the state of the chip into a `status` variable:

```
aci_evt_opcode_t status = BTLEserial.getState();
```

Then, if the status shows that some device is connect to the Bluetooth chip, we will handle any incoming requests:

```
if (status == ACI_EVT_CONNECTED) {
  rest.handle(BTLEserial);
}
```

Let's now see the details of the `servoControl` function that we will use to control the servo motor remotely. It simply takes a string as an input, containing the position that we want to apply on the servo motor:

```
int servoControl(String command) {

  // Get position from command
  int pos = command.toInt();
  Serial.println(pos);

  myservo.write(pos);

  return 1;
}
```

> Note that all the code for this chapter can be found inside the GitHub repository of the book at `https://github.com/marcoschwartz/arduino-android-blueprints`.

You can now upload the code to the Arduino board and move to the next section.

Setting up the Android app project

In this project, we will design a very simple Android app that will show the Bluetooth callback in a single-line text view and the sensor output in another text view. This time around, we will also implement a **Refresh** button, which will restart the Bluetooth callback if there is a need for a refresh.

The part of the project that will be more sophisticated is accessing the hardware sensors available for us in order to send commands to the Servo and rotate the shaft according to the x-axis orientation of our Android device, determined by the gyroscope hardware, which is included in the device.

It is important to note that sensor readings and data could vary between different Android devices due to different hardware setups. Then again, you could use this project as a baseline to further your ventures.

We will assume that you have switched on the `Auto-Import` function within your **Preferences** option. If not, kindly activate it by going to the **Auto-Import** preferences and selecting all the available options. The **Auto-Import** preferences are available on Mac and Windows as follows:

- On a Mac, Navigate to **Android Studio** | **Preferences** | **Editor** | **Auto-Import**.
- On Windows, Navigate to **File** | **Settings**| **Editor**| **Auto-Import**.

With all the necessary settings in place, we will first start off by creating a new project where we will choose the following within the **New Project** setup:

- **Name**: Android Gyroscope Servo Control
- **Minimum SDK**: `18`
- **Project**: `Blank Activity`
- **Activity Name**: `MainScreen`

In order to make this project work, we will need to first go over to the Android `Manifest` file, which is available at `app` > `src` > `main` > `AndroidManifest.xml`.

Laying out the Android user interface and permissions

Once we open the file, we will need to add permissions for access to Bluetooth and access to the gyroscope sensor hardware. The final Android `Manifest.xml` file will look as follows:

```
<?xml version="1.0" encoding="utf-8"?>
<manifest xmlns:android="http://schemas.android.com/apk/res/android"
    package="com.arduinoandroid.androidarduinosensserv" >

    <uses-permission android:name="android.hardware.sensor.
gyroscope"/>
    <uses-permission android:name="android.permission.BLUETOOTH"/>
    <uses-permission android:name="android.permission.BLUETOOTH_
ADMIN"/>

    <application
        android:allowBackup="true"
        android:icon="@drawable/ic_launcher"
        android:label="@string/app_name"
        android:theme="@style/AppTheme" >
        <activity
            android:name=".MainScreen"
            android:label="@string/app_name" >
            <intent-filter>
                <action android:name="android.intent.action.MAIN" />

                <category android:name="android.intent.category.
LAUNCHER" />
            </intent-filter>
        </activity>
    </application>

</manifest>
```

In this particular project, we will not put an emphasis on getting the user interface to be highly polished but instead, we will focus more on getting the orientation sensors to function appropriately with the servo motor.

In our project, we will navigate to the main layout file, which can be accessed by navigating to `app` > `src` > `res` > `layout` > `activity_main_screen.xml`.

The following code will implement a linear layout that has two `TextView` modules and a button. Go ahead and replace the current code in your project with the following:

```
<LinearLayout xmlns:android="http://schemas.android.com/apk/res/
android"
    android:layout_width="fill_parent"
    android:layout_height="fill_parent"
    android:orientation="vertical"
    android:weightSum="1">

    <TextView
        android:id="@+id/btView"
        android:layout_width="wrap_content"
        android:layout_height="wrap_content"
        android:layout_gravity="center_horizontal"
        android:layout_marginTop="80dp"
        android:text="bluetooth text"
        android:textAppearance="?android:attr/textAppearanceSmall" />

    <Button
        android:id="@+id/refreshButton"
        style="?android:attr/buttonStyleSmall"
        android:layout_width="wrap_content"
        android:layout_height="wrap_content"
        android:layout_gravity="center_horizontal"
        android:layout_marginTop="60dp"
        android:text="Refresh" />

    <TextView
        android:id="@+id/tv"
        android:layout_width="wrap_content"
        android:layout_height="wrap_content"
        android:layout_gravity="bottom|center_horizontal"
        android:layout_marginTop="250dp"
        android:text="Gyro output" />
</LinearLayout>
```

Setting up the app's internals

We will then move on to the `MainScreen.java` file, which is available at `app` > `src` > `main` > `java` > `package name` > `MainScreen.java`.

We will then replace the current code with the following code that we will walk through step-by-step and with **Auto-import** enabled; Android Studio will automatically import all the statements that we need for our project.

We start off by declaring the class that extends `Activity` and, in addition, we will need to add the capability for the Java class to implement `SensorEventListener`, which encompasses the main methods that are needed for detection of `sensor activity`:

```
public class MainScreen extends Activity implements
SensorEventListener {
```

The following are all the variables that need to be declared in order to work with the BLE module, log tag for logging purposes, user interface elements, handler methods, and Bluetooth characteristics:

```
    // UUIDs for UAT service and associated characteristics.
    public static UUID UART_UUID = UUID.fromString("6E400001-B5A3-
F393-E0A9-E50E24DCCA9E");
    public static UUID TX_UUID = UUID.fromString("6E400002-B5A3-F393-
E0A9-E50E24DCCA9E");
    public static UUID RX_UUID = UUID.fromString("6E400003-B5A3-F393-
E0A9-E50E24DCCA9E");
// UUID for the BTLE client characteristic which is necessary for
notifications.
    public static UUID CLIENT_UUID = UUID.fromString("00002902-0000-
1000-8000-00805f9b34fb");

    //Getting the name for Log Tags
    private final String LOG_TAG = MainScreen.class.getSimpleName();

    /**
     * Indicates which angle we are currently pointing the phone (and
hence servo) in:
     * -2: 0-45 degrees
     * -1: 45-90 degrees
     * 0: 90 degrees
     * 1: 90-135 degrees
     * 2: 135-180 degrees
     * <p/>
```

```
     * Default is the neutral position, i.e. 0.
     */
    int currentPosition = 0;

    long lastSensorChangedEventTimestamp = 0;

    //Declaring UI Elements
    private TextView gyroTextView;
    private TextView bluetoothTv;

    //Declaring SensorManager variables
    private SensorManager sensorManager;

    //Sensor Delay Methods
    int PERIOD = 1000000000; // read sensor data each second
    Handler handler;
    boolean canTransmitSensorData = false;
    boolean isHandlerLive = false;

    private boolean areServicesAccessible = false;
```

> The custom UART service for the Adafruit Bluetooth module uses the following UUIDs, which are the values you need to know to make our Android application talk to the appropriate characteristic. There is one characteristic for TX and another for RX, similar to the way that UART uses two lines to send and receive data as follows:
>
> **UART service UUID**: 6E400001-B5A3-F393-E0A9-E50E24DCCA9E
>
> **TX characteristic UUID**: 6E400002-B5A3-F393-E0A9-E50E24DCCA9E
>
> **RX characteristic UUID**: 6E400003-B5A3-F393-E0A9-E50E24DCCA9E

The Bluetooth logic that plays an important role in our project to deal with all the callbacks is available in its entirety in our GitHub repository. The main Java activity with all the Bluetooth logic is available at `http://git.io/XSHnow`.

In the following section of code, we will be declaring what will happen when the activity will be created and setting all the necessary functions to make the application logic connect to the layout files.

In the `onCreate()` method, we will also be initializing the `SensorManager` class, which will be needed to get access to the system's service.

```
@Override
public void onCreate(Bundle savedInstanceState) {
    super.onCreate(savedInstanceState);
    setContentView(R.layout.activity_main_screen);

    handler = new Handler();

    // Setup the refresh button
    final Button refreshButton = (Button) findViewById(R.
id.refreshButton);
    refreshButton.setOnClickListener(new View.OnClickListener() {
        @Override
        public void onClick(View view) {
            restartScan();
        }
    });

    //get the TextView from the layout file
    gyroTextView = (TextView) findViewById(R.id.tv);
    bluetoothTv = (TextView) findViewById(R.id.btView);

    //get a hook to the sensor service
    sensorManager = (SensorManager) getSystemService(SENSOR_
SERVICE);
}
```

In the `onStart()` method, we will use the `SensorManager` class to register the type of sensor that we will be using. In this case, we will be using the orientation sensors and setting `SENSOR_DELAY_NORMAL`, which we will need to modify later on so as to ensure that there is enough delay between each call. In the `onStart()` method, we will also be initializing the Bluetooth adapter to start listening for devices:

```
@Override
protected void onStart() {
    super.onResume();

    /*register the sensor listener to listen to the gyroscope
sensor, use the
    callbacks defined in this class, and gather the sensor
information as quick
```

```
        as possible*/
        sensorManager.registerListener(this,
                sensorManager.getDefaultSensor(Sensor.TYPE_
ORIENTATION),
                SensorManager.SENSOR_DELAY_NORMAL
        );

        //handler.post(processSensors);

        // Scan for all BTLE devices.
        // The first one with the UART service will be chosen--see the
code in the scanCallback.

        bluetoothAdaper = BluetoothAdapter.getDefaultAdapter();

        startScan();
    }
```

It's always important to unregister the sensor listener and disconnect the BLE connection when the app is closed so as to prevent the battery drain and device memory resources:

```
    //When this Activity isn't visible anymore
    @Override
    protected void onStop() {
        //unregister the sensor listener
        sensorManager.unregisterListener(this);
        //disconnect and close Bluetooth Connection for better
reliability
        if (gatt != null) {
            gatt.disconnect();
            gatt.close();
            gatt = null;
            tx = null;
            rx = null;
        }

        super.onStop();
        areServicesAccessible = false;
    }
```

The following code will deal with all the `Sensor` methods that need to be implemented in order to ensure there is enough delay between each sensor reading and to send the necessary commands to the Bluetooth-enabled Arduino for the servo motor to rotate the shaft according to the *x*-axis of the device:

```
    //SENSOR METHODS

    private final Runnable processSensors = new Runnable() {
        @Override
        public void run() {
            // Do work with the sensor values.
            canTransmitSensorData = !canTransmitSensorData;
            // The Runnable is posted to run again here:
            handler.postDelayed(this, PERIOD);
        }
    };

    @Override
    public void onAccuracyChanged(Sensor arg0, int arg1) {
        //Do nothing.
    }

    @Override
    public void onSensorChanged(SensorEvent event) {

        if ((event.accuracy != SensorManager.SENSOR_STATUS_UNRELIABLE)
                 && (event.timestamp - lastSensorChangedEventTimestamp
> PERIOD)) {

            System.out.println(event.timestamp -
lastSensorChangedEventTimestamp);
            lastSensorChangedEventTimestamp = event.timestamp;

            // Truncate to an integer, since precision loss is really
not a serious
            // matter here, and it will make it much easier (and
cheaper) to compare.
            // We will also log the integer values of [2]
            int xTilt = (int) event.values[2];
            int yTilt = (int) event.values[1];
            int zTilt = (int) event.values[0];
```

```
            gyroTextView.setText("Orientation X (Roll) :" + xTilt +
"\n" +
                    "Orientation Y (Pitch) :" + yTilt + "\n" +
                    "Orientation Z (Yaw) :" + zTilt);

            //Log.i(LOG_TAG, "The XTilt is:" + String.valueOf(xTilt));

            if (areServicesAccessible) {
                turnServoFinegrained(xTilt);
            }
        }
    }


    private void turnServoFinegrained(int xTilt) {

        // Default to vertical position
        int rotationAngle = 90;

        // Turn left
        if (xTilt > 0) {
            rotationAngle = 90 - xTilt;
        }

        // Turn right
        else {
            rotationAngle = 90 + Math.abs(xTilt);
        }

        String setServoMessage = "/servo?params=" + rotationAngle + "
/";
        tx.setValue(setServoMessage.getBytes(Charset.
forName("UTF-8")));
        if (gatt.writeCharacteristic(tx)) {
            writeSensorData("Sent: " + setServoMessage);
        } else {
            writeSensorData("Couldn't write TX characteristic!");
        }
    }
```

The following code will ensure that the commands that are sent to the BLE module are shown in the Bluetooth text output on our user interface layout:

```
        private void writeSensorData(final CharSequence text) {
            runOnUiThread(new Runnable() {
                @Override
                public void run() {
                    Log.e(LOG_TAG, text.toString());
                    //bluetoothTv = (TextView) findViewById(R.id.btView);
                    output = text.toString();
                    bluetoothTv.setText(output);
                }
            });
        }
    }
```

Once you've written all the code, which you can easily follow along on our GitHub repository, available at `https://github.com/marcoschwartz/arduino-android-blueprints/tree/master/chapter6`, make sure that you have a physical device that is running Android 4.3 or higher and Bluetooth switched on. Once you build the project, you should see something similar to the following screenshot:

How to go further

Orientation readings from the Android app can be further visualized in the app with real-time graphs, and this project could be further advanced and integrated into a remote object control app where the Android smartphone's user can control an object that is connected to the servo motor from a specific distance.

Simple yet useful application of such an action would be to open a gate or control a mobile robot via a gyroscope. Android smartphones also have a number of other sensors available for us, such as the accelerometer and magnetometer, which could effectively be used to control different components connected to the Arduino microcontroller.

Summary

Throughout this chapter, we learned how to take advantage of one of the most important sensors on the Android phone, the gyroscope sensor, to be able to control the Arduino-controlled servo motor. We achieve this communication and action via the BLE capabilities of the Arduino equipped with the Adafruit BLE module and the possibilities of the Android operating system running 4.3 or higher.

This chapter also provides the foundation steps to the following chapter, which will access one of the Android device's most important hardwares.

7

Voice-activated Arduino

In this chapter, we will use another feature of Android devices to control an Arduino system: voice recognition. We will control a relay that is connected to an Arduino board by sending vocal commands from the phone.

This relay can be connected to many things. For example, it can be connected to an electric door lock so that you could open and close a door by just speaking into your phone. You can also connect the relay to a lamp, to switch the lamp on and off by giving a vocal command to your phone.

In this chapter, you will learn how to:

- Connect a relay and a Bluetooth module to an Arduino board so that it can be controlled from the Android application
- Build an application using the Android speech API
- Control the relay on the Arduino board by voice

Hardware and software requirements

The first thing you will need for this project is an Arduino Uno board.

Then you will need a BLE module. We chose the Adafruit nRF8001 chip because it comes with a nice Arduino library and it has already existing examples of Android apps to control the module.

You will also need a relay module. For this project, we used a 5V relay module from Polulu, which is the same as the one we used in the previous chapters. This is an image of the relay we used for this chapter:

Finally, to make the different electrical connections, you will also need a breadboard and some jumper wires.

This is the list of all hardware parts you will need for this project, along with links to find these parts on the Web:

- The Arduino Uno board (`http://www.adafruit.com/product/50`)
- The 5V relay module (`http://www.pololu.com/product/2480`)
- The Adafruit nRF8001 breakout board (`https://www.adafruit.com/products/1697`)
- The breadboard (`https://www.adafruit.com/product/64`)
- Jumper wires (`https://www.adafruit.com/product/758`)

Note that these are all the components we already used in the previous chapters.

On the software side, you will need the following:

- The Arduino IDE (`http://arduino.cc/en/Main/Software`)
- The Arduino aREST library (`https://github.com/marcoschwartz/aREST/`)
- The nRF8001 Arduino library for the BLE chip (`https://github.com/adafruit/Adafruit_nRF8001`)

To install a given library, simply extract the folder in your `Arduino/libraries` folder (or create this folder if it doesn't exist yet).

Configuring the hardware

We will now build the hardware part of the project. To help you out, the following is the schematic of the project, without the relay being connected yet:

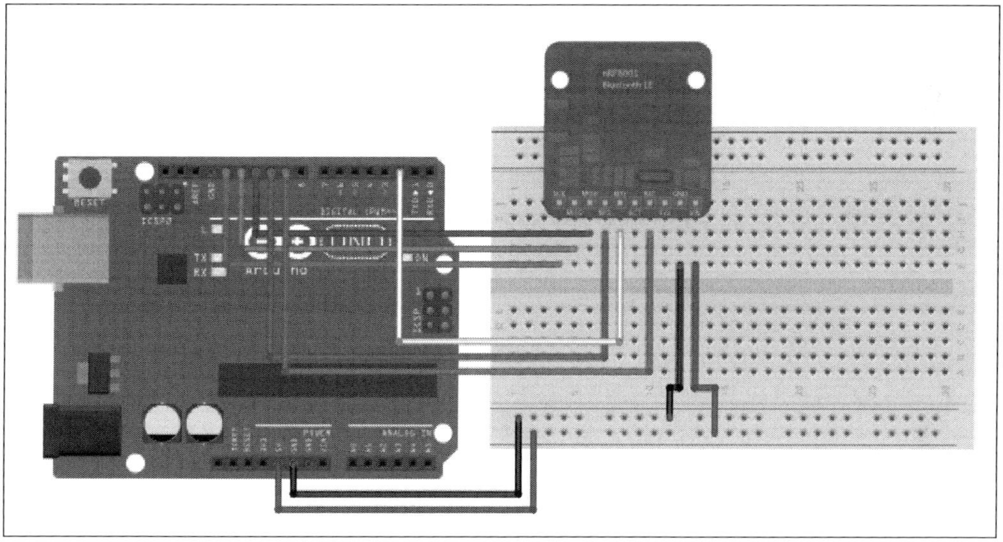

Note that these instructions are the same as in the previous chapter. Therefore, you can just use the same configuration if you still have it built on your desk.

The first step is to place the Bluetooth module on the breadboard. Then, connect the power supply from the Arduino board to the breadboard: 5V of the Arduino board goes to the red power rail and **GND** goes to the blue power rail.

We will now connect the BLE module. First, connect the power supply of the module: **GND** goes to the blue power rail, and **VIN** goes to the red power rail. After this, you need to connect the different wires responsible for the SPI interface: **SCK** to Arduino pin **13**, **MISO** to Arduino pin **12**, and **MOSI** to Arduino pin **11**. Then connect the **REQ** pin to Arduino pin **10**. Finally, connect the **RDY** pin to Arduino pin **2**, and the **RST** pin to Arduino pin **9**.

For the relay module, connect the **VCC** pin to the red power rail on the breadboard and the **GND** pin on the blue power rail. Finally, connect the **SIG** pin of the relay to pin number **7** of the Arduino board.

The following is an image of an overview of the assembled project (for the precise connections between the elements, refer to the preceding instructions):

The close-up image of the relay and BLE module can be seen as follows:

Writing the Arduino sketch

We will now write the sketch to control the relay from an Android device. Note that this is the same sketch as in the previous chapter, so you can skip it if you already did this part for the last chapter. The following is the complete sketch for this part:

```
// Control Arduino board from BLE

// Libraries
#include <SPI.h>
#include "Adafruit_BLE_UART.h"
#include <aREST.h>
```

```
// Pins
#define ADAFRUITBLE_REQ 10
#define ADAFRUITBLE_RDY 2    // Should be pin 2 or 3
#define ADAFRUITBLE_RST 9

// Relay pin
const int relay_pin = 7;

// Create aREST instance
aREST rest = aREST();

// BLE instance
Adafruit_BLE_UART BTLEserial = Adafruit_BLE_UART(ADAFRUITBLE_REQ,
ADAFRUITBLE_RDY, ADAFRUITBLE_RST);

void setup(void)
{
  // Start Serial
  Serial.begin(115200);

  // Start BLE
  BTLEserial.begin();

  // Give name and ID to device
  rest.set_id("001");
  rest.set_name("relay_control");

   // Init relay pin
  pinMode(relay_pin,OUTPUT);
}

void loop() {

  // Tell the nRF8001 to do whatever it should be working on.
  BTLEserial.pollACI();

  // Ask what is our current status
  aci_evt_opcode_t status = BTLEserial.getState();

  // Handle REST calls
  if (status == ACI_EVT_CONNECTED) {
    rest.handle(BTLEserial);
  }
 }
```

Now, let's see the details of the sketch. It starts by importing the required libraries for the nRF8001 module and the aREST library:

```
#include <SPI.h>
#include "Adafruit_BLE_UART.h"
#include <aREST.h>
```

Then we will define which pin the BLE module is connected to:

```
#define ADAFRUITBLE_REQ 10
#define ADAFRUITBLE_RDY 2     // This should be an interrupt pin, on
Uno thats #2 or #3
#define ADAFRUITBLE_RST 9
```

We also need to declare which pin the relay is connected to:

```
const int relay_pin = 7;
```

After this, we can create an instance of the aREST API that will be used to handle the requests coming via Bluetooth:

```
aREST rest = aREST();
```

We will also create an instance of the nRF8001 chip library:

```
Adafruit_BLE_UART BTLEserial = Adafruit_BLE_UART(ADAFRUITBLE_REQ,
ADAFRUITBLE_RDY, ADAFRUITBLE_RST);
```

Now, in the `setup()` function of the sketch, we will initialize serial communications and print a welcome message as follows:

```
BTLEserial.begin();
```

We will also give a name to the device:

```
rest.set_id("001");
rest.set_name("relay_control");
```

Finally, we will set the relay pin so it becomes an output:

```
pinMode(relay_pin,OUTPUT);
```

Now, in the `loop()` function of the sketch, we will check the status of the BLE chip:

```
BTLEserial.pollACI();
aci_evt_opcode_t status = BTLEserial.getState();
```

Then, if any device is connected to the chip, we will process any incoming request with the aREST library:

```
if (status == ACI_EVT_CONNECTED) {
  rest.handle(BTLEserial);
}
```

Note that all the code for this chapter can be found in the GitHub repository of the book at `https://github.com/marcoschwartz/arduino-android-blueprints`.

It's now time to upload the sketch to your Arduino board. When this is done, you can move on to the development of the Android app to control the Arduino board via the BLE sketch.

Setting up the Android app

In this project, we will be implementing an Android app that leverages the use of the Speech Recognition API and we are going output that text in an `EditText` field. In the background, we will also include the BLE services in order to connect to the BLE module and be able to send messages to it. Once we have the BLE and Speech Recognition API set up, we will be able to connect them both by setting up conditions where if the speech is recognized as `switch on`, it will switch on the relay, whereas if `switch off` is recognized, the relay will be switched off.

We will assume that you will switch on the `Auto-Import` function within your preferences. If not, kindly activate it by going to the **Auto-Import** preferences and selecting all the available options. The **Auto-Import** preferences are available on Mac and Windows as follows:

- On a Mac, navigate to **Android Studio** > **Preferences** > **Editor** > **Auto-Import**
- On Windows, navigate to **File** > **Settings** > **Editor** > **Auto-Import**

With all the necessary settings in place, we will first start off by creating a new project where we will choose the following within the **New Project** setup:

- **Name**: `Talk to Arduino`
- **Minimum SDK**: `18`
- **Project**: `Blank Activity`
- **Activity Name**: `MainScreen`
- **Domain**: `arduinoandroid.com`

In order to make this project work, we will need to first go over to the Android `Manifest` file, which is available at `app` > `src` > `main` > `AndroidManifest.xml`.

Laying out the Android user interface and permissions

Once we open the file, we need to add permissions for access to Bluetooth functionality; this will allow us to transmit the voice messages to the Arduino. The following two lines of XML need to be added to the Android `Manifest` file:

```
    <uses-permission android:name="android.permission.BLUETOOTH"/>
    <uses-permission android:name="android.permission.BLUETOOTH_
ADMIN"/>
```

The next step that we will take is to set up the very basic Android layout file so that we are able to implement the app's functions and to allow the user to activate the voice recognition intent.

In our project, we will navigate to the main layout file, which can be accessed from `app` > `src` > `res` > `layout` > `activity_speech.xml`.

By replacing the current code with the following, we will add a relative layout with two buttons, an `EditText` field and a `TextView` field, which will allow us to see the outcome of our voice input:

```
<RelativeLayout xmlns:android="http://schemas.android.com/apk/res/
android"
    xmlns:tools="http://schemas.android.com/tools"
    android:layout_width="match_parent"
    android:layout_height="match_parent"
    android:paddingLeft="@dimen/activity_horizontal_margin"
    android:paddingRight="@dimen/activity_horizontal_margin"
    android:paddingTop="@dimen/activity_vertical_margin"
    android:paddingBottom="@dimen/activity_vertical_margin"
    tools:context=".SpeechActivity">

    <Button
        android:layout_width="wrap_content"
        android:layout_height="wrap_content"
        android:text="Talk to Arduino"
        android:id="@+id/talktoArduino"
        android:layout_centerVertical="true"
        android:layout_centerHorizontal="true" />

    <EditText
        android:layout_width="wrap_content"
        android:layout_height="wrap_content"
```

```
        android:id="@+id/recordedTalk"
        android:text="What is recorded will be written here"
        android:layout_alignParentBottom="true"
        android:layout_centerHorizontal="true"
        android:layout_marginBottom="139dp" />

    <TextView
        android:layout_width="wrap_content"
        android:layout_height="wrap_content"
        android:textAppearance="?android:attr/textAppearanceSmall"
        android:text="Bluetooth Output"
        android:id="@+id/btView"
        android:layout_marginTop="76dp"
        android:layout_alignParentTop="true"
        android:layout_centerHorizontal="true" />

    <Button
        android:layout_width="wrap_content"
        android:layout_height="wrap_content"
        android:text="Refresh"
        android:id="@+id/refreshBtn"
        android:layout_above="@+id/talktoArduino"
        android:layout_alignStart="@+id/talktoArduino"
        android:layout_alignEnd="@+id/talktoArduino" />
</RelativeLayout>
```

Coding the app's internals

We will then move on to the `MainScreen.java` file, which is available at `app` > `src` > `main` > `java` > `package name` > `MainScreen.java`.

We will then replace the current code with the following code, which we will walk through step-by-step and with **Auto-import** enabled; Android Studio will automatically import all the statements that we will need for our project.

> Feel free to follow along the project through the GitHub repository where all the source is available for the users of our book in its entirety. The repository is available at `https://github.com/marcoschwartz/arduino-android-blueprints/tree/master/chapter7/TalktoArduino`.

We will start off by declaring the class that extends `Activity`:

```
public class SpeechActivity extends Activity {
```

The following are all the variables that are needed to be declared in order to work with the BLE module, log tag for logging purposes, user interface elements, and Bluetooth characteristics for voice recognition requests:

```
    private static final int VOICE_RECOGNITION_REQUEST = 1;

    //Getting the name for Log Tags
    private final String LOG_TAG = SpeechActivity.class.
getSimpleName();

    //Declare U.I Elements
    private Button startTalk;
    private Button refresh;
    private EditText speechInput;
    private TextView btv;

    // UUIDs for UAT service and associated characteristics.
    public static UUID UART_UUID = UUID.fromString("6E400001-B5A3-
F393-E0A9-E50E24DCCA9E");
    public static UUID TX_UUID = UUID.fromString("6E400002-B5A3-F393-
E0A9-E50E24DCCA9E");
    public static UUID RX_UUID = UUID.fromString("6E400003-B5A3-F393-
E0A9-E50E24DCCA9E");
    // UUID for the BTLE client characteristic which is necessary for
notifications.
    public static UUID CLIENT_UUID = UUID.fromString("00002902-0000-
1000-8000-00805f9b34fb");

    // BTLE stateta
    private BluetoothAdapter adapter;
    private BluetoothGatt gatt;
    private BluetoothGattCharacteristic tx;
    private BluetoothGattCharacteristic rx;

    private boolean areServicesAccessible = false;
```

In the `onCreate()` method, we will initialize the user interface layout that we implemented earlier and connect the user interface elements to the different methods within our code:

```
@Override
protected void onCreate(Bundle savedInstanceState) {
    super.onCreate(savedInstanceState);
    setContentView(R.layout.activity_speech);
    startTalk = (Button) findViewById(R.id.talktoArduino);
    refresh = (Button) findViewById(R.id.refreshBtn);
    speechInput = (EditText) findViewById(R.id.recordedTalk);
    btv = (TextView) findViewById(R.id.btView);


    startTalk.setOnClickListener(new View.OnClickListener() {
        @Override
        public void onClick(View view) {
            recordSpeech();
        }
    });

    refresh.setOnClickListener(new View.OnClickListener() {
        @Override
        public void onClick(View view) {
            restartScan();
        }
    });

}
```

The `recordSpeech()` method allows us to launch the Google speech recognition intent where we can modify the message that we will show the user. In this case, we decided to replace the default text with the prompt, "You can now send a command to the Arduino":

```
public void recordSpeech() {

        Intent intent = new Intent(RecognizerIntent.ACTION_RECOGNIZE_
SPEECH);

        intent.putExtra(RecognizerIntent.EXTRA_LANGUAGE_MODEL,
RecognizerIntent.LANGUAGE_MODEL_FREE_FORM);
```

```
        intent.putExtra(RecognizerIntent.EXTRA_PROMPT, "You can now
send a command to the Arduino");

        startActivityForResult(intent, VOICE_RECOGNITION_REQUEST);
    }
```

The `onActivityResult()` method allows the application to process what has been recognized and implement methods based on what has been received. In the following method, we will take the speech that has been recognized, output it in the `EditText` field that we set up earlier and, depending on the output, we will send the commands via BLE to switch on or switch off the relay:

```
    @Override

    protected void onActivityResult(int requestCode, int resultCode,
Intent data) {

        if (requestCode == VOICE_RECOGNITION_REQUEST && resultCode ==
RESULT_OK) {

            ArrayList<String> matches = data.getStringArrayListExtra(R
ecognizerIntent.EXTRA_RESULTS);

            String userInput = matches.get(0);

            TextView textSaid = (TextView) findViewById(R.
id.recordedTalk);

            textSaid.setText(matches.get(0));

            //add an if else loop or case statement

            if (userInput.equalsIgnoreCase("switch on")) {
                String setOutputMessage = "/digital/7/1 /";
                tx.setValue(setOutputMessage.getBytes(Charset.
forName("UTF-8")));
                if (gatt.writeCharacteristic(tx)) {
                    writeSensorData("Sent: " + setOutputMessage);
                } else {
                    writeSensorData("Couldn't write TX
characteristic!");
                }
```

```
            } else if (userInput.equalsIgnoreCase("switch off")) {
                String setOutputMessage = "/digital/7/0 /";
                tx.setValue(setOutputMessage.getBytes(Charset.
forName("UTF-8")));
                if (gatt.writeCharacteristic(tx)) {
                    writeSensorData("Sent: " + setOutputMessage);
                } else {
                    writeSensorData("Couldn't write TX
characteristic!");
                }
            }

        }
        super.onActivityResult(requestCode, resultCode, data);
    }
```

The following code deals with making sure the Bluetooth callback output is being sent to its associated `TextView`:

```
    private void writeSensorData(final CharSequence text) {
        Log.e(LOG_TAG, text.toString());
        btv.setText(text.toString());
    }
```

Here, we will deal with all the `BluetoothGattCallback` class that needs to be implemented to connect to the BLE module:

```
    // BTLE device scanning bluetoothGattCallback.

    // Main BTLE device bluetoothGattCallback where much of the logic
occurs.
    private BluetoothGattCallback bluetoothGattCallback = new
BluetoothGattCallback() {
        // Called whenever the device connection state changes, i.e.
from disconnected to connected.
        @Override
        public void onConnectionStateChange(BluetoothGatt gatt, int
status, int newState) {
            super.onConnectionStateChange(gatt, status, newState);
            if (newState == BluetoothGatt.STATE_CONNECTED) {
                writeSensorData("Connected!");
                // Discover services.
                if (!gatt.discoverServices()) {
```

```
                    writeSensorData("Failed to start discovering
services!");
                }
            } else if (newState == BluetoothGatt.STATE_DISCONNECTED) {
                writeSensorData("Disconnected!");
            } else {
                writeSensorData("Connection state changed.  New state:
" + newState);
            }
        }

        // Called when services have been discovered on the remote
device.
        // It seems to be necessary to wait for this discovery to
occur before
        // manipulating any services or characteristics.
        public void onServicesDiscovered(BluetoothGatt gatt, int
status) {
            super.onServicesDiscovered(gatt, status);
            if (status == BluetoothGatt.GATT_SUCCESS) {
                writeSensorData("Service discovery completed!");
            } else {
                writeSensorData("Service discovery failed with status:
" + status);
            }
            // Save reference to each characteristic.
            tx = gatt.getService(UART_UUID).getCharacteristic(TX_
UUID);
            rx = gatt.getService(UART_UUID).getCharacteristic(RX_
UUID);

            // Setup notifications on RX characteristic changes (i.e.
data received).
            // First call setCharacteristicNotification to enable
notification.
            if (!gatt.setCharacteristicNotification(rx, true)) {
                writeSensorData("Couldn't set notifications for RX
characteristic!");
            }

            // Next update the RX characteristic's client descriptor
to enable notifications.
```

```
            if (rx.getDescriptor(CLIENT_UUID) != null) {
                BluetoothGattDescriptor desc =
rx.getDescriptor(CLIENT_UUID);
                desc.setValue(BluetoothGattDescriptor.ENABLE_
NOTIFICATION_VALUE);
                if (!gatt.writeDescriptor(desc)) {
                    writeSensorData("Couldn't write RX client
descriptor value!");
                }
            } else {
                writeSensorData("Couldn't get RX client descriptor!");
            }
            areServicesAccessible = true;
        }
    };
```

In the following `onStart()` and `onStop()` methods, we are making sure that we start scanning of BLE devices and that Bluetooth scanning stops when we close the application so as to prevent the battery drain and ensure optimization of device memory resources for tasks running in the foreground:

```
    protected void onStart() {
        Log.d(LOG_TAG,"onStart has been called");
        super.onStart();
        // / Scan for all BTLE devices.
        // The first one with the UART service will be chosen--see the
code in the scanCallback.
        adapter = BluetoothAdapter.getDefaultAdapter();
        startScan();
    }

    //When this Activity isn't visible anymore
    protected void onStop() {
        Log.d(LOG_TAG,"onStop has been called");
        //disconnect and close Bluetooth Connection for better
reliability
        if (gatt != null) {
            gatt.disconnect();
            gatt.close();
            gatt = null;
            tx = null;
            rx = null;
        }
        super.onStop();
    }
```

The following methods deal with the starting, stopping, and restarting of the Bluetooth scan callback:

```
    private void startScan() {
        if (!adapter.isEnabled()) {
            adapter.enable();
        }
        if (!adapter.isDiscovering()) {
            adapter.startDiscovery();
        }
        writeSensorData("Scanning for devices...");
        adapter.startLeScan(scanCallback);
    }

    private void stopScan() {
        if (adapter.isDiscovering()) {
            adapter.cancelDiscovery();
        }
        writeSensorData("Stopping scan");
        adapter.stopLeScan(scanCallback);
    }

    private void restartScan() {
        stopScan();
        startScan();
    }
```

The `scanCallback()` method is concerned mostly with the main logic to get the Bluetooth device addresses and maintain the necessary connections between the Android device and BLE module:

```
    /**
     * Main callback following an LE device scan
     */
    private BluetoothAdapter.LeScanCallback scanCallback = new
BluetoothAdapter.LeScanCallback() {
        // Called when a device is found.
        @Override
        public void onLeScan(BluetoothDevice bluetoothDevice, int i,
byte[] bytes) {
            Log.d(LOG_TAG, bluetoothDevice.getAddress());

            writeSensorData("Found device: " + bluetoothDevice.
getAddress());
```

```
            // Check if the device has the UART service.
            if (BluetoothUtils.parseUUIDs(bytes).contains(UART_UUID))
{
                // Found a device, stop the scan.
                adapter.stopLeScan(scanCallback);
                writeSensorData("Found UART service!");
                // Connect to the device.
                // Control flow will now go to the
bluetoothGattCallback functions when BTLE events occur.
                gatt = bluetoothDevice.connectGatt(getApplicationConte
xt(), false, bluetoothGattCallback);
            }
        }
    };
}
```

In contrast to the previous chapters of the book, you will recognize that we have transferred the UUID parsing to a `utility` class in order to refactor the code and make our code more readable. In order to create a `utility` class, we first need to right-click on our package name and create a new package and call it `Bluetooth`.

After this, we will right-click on the new package, select **New > Java Class**, and name the new class as `BluetoothUtils`.

After those two steps, we will replace the code within the class with the following code:

```
public class BluetoothUtils {

    // Filtering by custom UUID is broken in Android 4.3 and 4.4, see:
    //   http://stackoverflow.com/questions/18019161/startlescan-with-
128-bit-uuids-doesnt-work-on-native-android-ble-implementation?noredir
ect=1#comment27879874_18019161
    // This is a workaround function from the SO thread to manually
parse advertisement data.
    public static List<UUID> parseUUIDs(final byte[] advertisedData) {
        List<UUID> uuids = new ArrayList<UUID>();

        int offset = 0;
        while (offset < (advertisedData.length - 2)) {
            int len = advertisedData[offset++];
            if (len == 0)
                break;
```

```
            int type = advertisedData[offset++];
            switch (type) {
                case 0x02: // Partial list of 16-bit UUIDs
                case 0x03: // Complete list of 16-bit UUIDs
                    while (len > 1) {
                        int uuid16 = advertisedData[offset++];
                        uuid16 += (advertisedData[offset++] << 8);
                        len -= 2;
                        uuids.add(UUID.fromString(String.format("%08x-
0000-1000-8000-00805f9b34fb", uuid16)));
                    }
                    break;
                case 0x06:// Partial list of 128-bit UUIDs
                case 0x07:// Complete list of 128-bit UUIDs
                    // Loop through the advertised 128-bit UUID's.
                    while (len >= 16) {
                        try {
                            // Wrap the advertised bits and order
them.
                            ByteBuffer buffer = ByteBuffer.
wrap(advertisedData, offset++, 16).order(ByteOrder.LITTLE_ENDIAN);
                            long mostSignificantBit = buffer.
getLong();
                            long leastSignificantBit = buffer.
getLong();
                            uuids.add(new UUID(leastSignificantBit,
                                    mostSignificantBit));
                        } catch (IndexOutOfBoundsException e) {
                            // Defensive programming.
                            //Log.e(LOG_TAG, e.toString());
                            continue;
                        } finally {
                            // Move the offset to read the next uuid.
                            offset += 15;
                            len -= 16;
                        }
                    }
                    break;
                default:
                    offset += (len - 1);
                    break;
            }
        }
        return uuids;
    }
}
```

Once you have included this code, you can go ahead and build and run this app on your Android physical device, which is running Android 4.3 or higher and connected to the Internet, due to the fact that most of the speech recognition services work via the Internet.

When you load the app, you should start off with something as follows:

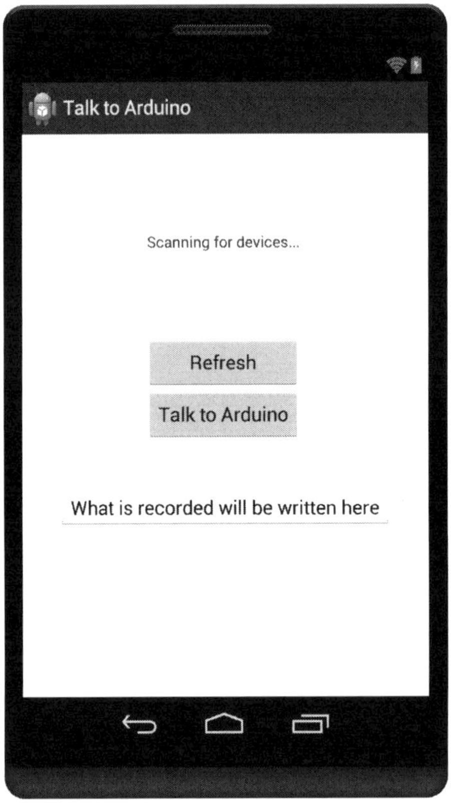

How to go further

This base project offers endless possibilities and you can possibly include other commands that can be recognized and connect other components and sensors in order to enhance the capabilities of your voice-activated app. We hope that with this baseline project, we can inspire you to enhance your projects further on.

Summary

Let's summarize what we did in this chapter. As usual, we connected a BLE module to our Arduino board so that it can receive commands via the Android phone. We also connected a simple relay module to the board, to control it via an Android application. Then we designed an application using the Android speech engine to control the relay depending on what the user says to the Android phone.

In the next chapter, we will use another feature of the Android phone to control Arduino projects: NFC. We will use NFC to control the state of a relay just by putting our phone in front of an Arduino NFC shield.

8
Control an Arduino Board via NFC

In this chapter, we will see the capabilities of integrating the Arduino **Near Field Communications** (**NFC**) shield from Seeed Studio with an NFC-enabled Android application that uses the **Android Beam** technology to send a message from the Android app to the NFC shield antenna. NFC allows instant communication between two devices that are close to each other, which makes it the perfect technology to open door locks or for payment services.

We will make a home automation application in this chapter. The NFC shield will be connected to the Arduino Uno board, along with the relay. Therefore, we will be able to switch the relay on or off depending on the message sent by the Android application.

This baseline project will help you develop interesting projects that use NFC and will potentially expand the capabilities of such a project.

The following will be the major takeaways from this chapter:

- Connecting an NFC shield to an Arduino board
- Building an Android app to communicate with the NFC Arduino shield
- Opening and closing a relay from an Android device via NFC

Hardware and software requirements

The first thing you will need for this project is an Arduino Uno board.

Then, you need an NFC shield. There are many NFC shields available on the market, but for this project, we chose an NFC shield V2.0 from SeeedStudio. We made this choice as the shield has good documentation and because some example code was already available.

You will also need a relay module. For this project, we used a 5V relay module from Polulu.

Finally, to make the different electrical connections, you will need some jumper wires.

The following is the list of all hardware parts you will need for this project, along with links to find these parts on the Web:

- The Arduino Uno board (`http://www.adafruit.com/product/50`)
- The 5V relay module (`http://www.pololu.com/product/2480`)
- The Arduino NFC shield (`http://www.seeedstudio.com/depot/nfc-shield-v20-p-1370.html`)
- The breadboard (`https://www.adafruit.com/product/64`)
- Jumper wires (`https://www.adafruit.com/product/758`)

On the software side, you will of course need the Arduino IDE. You will also need the following libraries to make the NFC chip work:

1. First, download the PN532 library (`https://github.com/Seeed-Studio/PN532`) and put all the folders into your Arduino's `libraries` folder.
2. Then, download the NDEF library (`https://github.com/don/NDEF`), and put it in your Arduino's `libraries` folder and rename the folder to `NDEF`.

Configuring the hardware

Now, let's assemble the project. The first step is to simply put the NFC shield on top of the Arduino Uno board, and to connect the NFC reader to the shield. Note that the NFC can come without the header being soldered; in this case, you will need to solder the headers on the shield yourself. To assemble the NFC reader to the shield, simply connect the reader via the antenna connector on the shield.

Now, let's connect the relay. Simply connect the relay module **VCC** pin to the 5V pin of the Arduino board, and the **GND** pin to the **GND** pin of the board. Finally, connect the **SIG** pin of the relay to pin number **8** of the Arduino board.

The following is what you should end up with:

Testing the NFC shield

Before writing the application to control the relay via NFC, we will first make sure that the shield is functional and that all the libraries were correctly installed. To do so, we will write a simple Arduino sketch. The following is the complete code for this part:

```
#include <SPI.h>
#include <PN532_SPI.h>
#include <PN532.h>
#include <NfcAdapter.h>

// NFC instances
PN532_SPI pn532spi(SPI, 10);
NfcAdapter nfc = NfcAdapter(pn532spi);

void setup(void) {

  // Start Serial
  Serial.begin(9600);

  // Start NFC chip
  Serial.println("NFC shield started");
  nfc.begin();
}
```

```
void loop(void) {

  // Start scan
  Serial.println("\nScan a NFC tag\n");
  if (nfc.tagPresent())
  {
    NfcTag tag = nfc.read();
    tag.print();
  }
  delay(5000);
}
```

Let's now look at the details of this sketch. It starts by including the required libraries:

```
#include <SPI.h>
#include <PN532_SPI.h>
#include <PN532.h>
#include <NfcAdapter.h>
```

Then, we can create an instance of the NFC adapter with these two lines of code:

```
PN532_SPI pn532spi(SPI, 10);
NfcAdapter nfc = NfcAdapter(pn532spi);
```

Now, in the `setup()` function of the sketch, we will initialize the serial communications:

```
Serial.begin(9600);
```

We will also start the NFC chip, and print a message on the serial monitor:

```
nfc.begin();
Serial.println("NFC shield started");
```

Now, in the `loop()` function of the sketch, we will check if an NFC tag is present, and we will read it if this is the case:

```
if (nfc.tagPresent())
{
  NfcTag tag = nfc.read();
  tag.print();
}
  delay(5000);
}
```

[Note that all the code for this chapter can be found in the GitHub repository of the book at `https://github.com/marcoschwartz/arduino-android-blueprints`.]

You can now upload the sketch to the Arduino board and open the serial monitor. You should see that the NFC chip is being initialized, and then it starts checking for available tags. If you have a simple NFC tag, you can test it now.

As an example, you can also use a simple tag from SeeedStudio (`http://www.seeedstudio.com/depot/MifareOne-RFID-Tag-1356MHz-p-923.html`).

These kinds of tags are actually simpler than the actual RFID technology, but they will work just fine to test our project.

Writing the Arduino sketch

We will now write the code that will receive commands from the Android NFC app. The goal of this code will be to switch the relay on or off when the NFC shield receives a given code from the Android device. As the code for this part is quite long, we will split the code into several parts that will be detailed individually.

The code starts by including the required libraries:

```
#include "SPI.h"
#include "PN532_SPI.h"
#include "snep.h"
#include "NdefMessage.h"
```

We will also define on which pin the relay is connected:

```
#define RELAY_PIN 8
```

After this, we will define the code that should be received from the Android app to switch the relay on or off:

```
#define RELAY_ON "oWnHV6uXre"
```

We will also need to create an instance of the NFC chip:

```
PN532_SPI pn532spi(SPI, 10);
SNEP nfc(pn532spi);
```

To store data coming from the Android phone via NFC, we will create a `char` buffer:

```
uint8_t ndefBuf[128];
```

In the `setup()` function of the sketch, we will start the serial communications:

```
Serial.begin(9600);
Serial.println("NFC Peer to Peer Light Switch");
```

We will also declare the relay pin as an output:

```
pinMode(RELAY_PIN, OUTPUT);
```

Now, in the `loop()` function, we will constantly check for data coming from the phone via NFC:

```
Serial.println("Waiting for message from Peer");
int msgSize = nfc.read(ndefBuf, sizeof(ndefBuf));
```

Now, if the message has a size different from zero, we store it, process it, and then check if it contains the correct key that we defined before. If this is the case, we will switch the state of the relay. The following piece of code does exactly the same:

```
if (msgSize > 0) {

    // Read message
    NdefMessage message  = NdefMessage(ndefBuf, msgSize);

    // Make sure there is at least one NDEF Record
    if (message.getRecordCount() > 0) {

      NdefRecord record = message.getRecord(0);
      Serial.println("Got first record");

      // Check the TNF and Record Type
      if (record.getTnf() == TNF_MIME_MEDIA && record.getType() ==
"application/com.arduinoandroid.arduinonfc") {
        Serial.println("Type is OK");

        // Get the bytes from the payload
        int payloadLength = record.getPayloadLength();
        byte payload[payloadLength];
        record.getPayload(payload);

        // Convert the payload to a String
        String payloadAsString = "";
        for (int c = 0; c < payloadLength; c++) {
          payloadAsString += (char)payload[c];
        }
```

```
        // Print out the data on the Serial monitor
        Serial.print("Payload is ");Serial.println(payloadAsString);

        // Modify the state of the light, based on the tag contents
        if (payloadAsString == RELAY_ON) {
            digitalWrite(RELAY_PIN, HIGH);
        } else {
            digitalWrite(RELAY_PIN, LOW);
        }
      } else {
        Serial.print("Expecting TNF 'Mime Media' (0x02) with type
'application/com.arduinoandroid.arduinonfc' but found TNF ");
        Serial.print(record.getTnf(), HEX);
        Serial.print(" type ");
        Serial.println(record.getType());
      }
    }
  }
}
```

Note that all the code for this chapter can be found in the GitHub repository of the book at `https://github.com/marcoschwartz/arduino-android-blueprints`.

You can now upload the code to the Arduino board, and move on to the development of the Android application.

Setting up the Android app

In this project, we will be implementing an Android app that leverages the use of the NFC API and hardware allowing us to send a MIME-type message to switch on and switch off the relay.

We will assume that you will have switched on the `Auto-Import` function within your preferences. If not, activate it by going to the **Auto-Import** preferences and selecting all available options. The **Auto-Import** preferences are available on Mac and Windows as follows:

- On a Mac, navigate to **Android Studio** > **Preferences** | **Editor** | **Auto-Import**
- On Windows, navigate to **File** | **Settings** > **Editor** > **Auto-Import**

With all the necessary settings in place, we will first start off by creating a new project, where we will choose the following within the **New Project** setup:

- **Name**: `Arduino NFC`
- **Minimum SDK**: `18`
- **Project**: `Blank Activity`
- **Activity Name**: MainScreen
- **Domain**: `arduinoandroid.com`

In order to make this project work, we will need to first go over to the Android `Manifest` file, which is available at `app` > `src` > `main` > `AndroidManifest.xml`.

Laying out the Android user interface and permissions

Once we open the file, we need to add permissions for the Android application to be able to access the NFC hardware. We will need to add the following two lines of code to our `AndroidManifest.xml` file in order to access both the user permissions and the actual NFC hardware:

```
<uses-permission android:name="android.permission.NFC" />
<uses-feature android:name="android.hardware.nfc"
android:required="true" />
```

The next step is to set up the basic Android layout file. This will allow us to implement a user interface consisting of two buttons (switch on and off) and a text view.

The text within the TextView will be the message that we will be sending to our NFC shield. The first step will be to navigate to the Android layout file, which is available at `app` > `src` > `res` > `layout` > `activity_nfc.xml`.

Once we are within this layout file, we will switch to the text view of the Android layout file, and we will replace the current code with the following lines of code:

```
<RelativeLayout xmlns:android="http://schemas.android.com/apk/res/
android"
    xmlns:tools="http://schemas.android.com/tools"
    android:layout_width="match_parent"
    android:layout_height="match_parent"
    android:paddingLeft="@dimen/activity_horizontal_margin"
    android:paddingRight="@dimen/activity_horizontal_margin"
    android:paddingTop="@dimen/activity_vertical_margin"
```

```
    android:paddingBottom="@dimen/activity_vertical_margin"
    tools:context=".NFCActivity">

    <TextView
        android:text="NFC Status"
        android:layout_width="wrap_content"
        android:layout_height="wrap_content"
        android:id="@+id/nfcTextStatus"
        android:layout_marginTop="83dp"
        android:layout_alignParentTop="true"
        android:layout_centerHorizontal="true" />

    <Button
        android:layout_width="wrap_content"
        android:layout_height="wrap_content"
        android:text="Switch On"
        android:id="@+id/switchOnBtn"
        android:layout_marginTop="59dp"
        android:layout_below="@+id/nfcTextStatus"
        android:layout_toLeftOf="@+id/nfcTextStatus"
        android:layout_toStartOf="@+id/nfcTextStatus" />

    <Button
        android:layout_width="wrap_content"
        android:layout_height="wrap_content"
        android:text="Switch Off"
        android:id="@+id/switchOffBtn"
        android:layout_alignTop="@+id/switchOnBtn"
        android:layout_toRightOf="@+id/nfcTextStatus"
        android:layout_toEndOf="@+id/nfcTextStatus" />

    <TextView
        android:layout_width="wrap_content"
        android:layout_height="wrap_content"
        android:textAppearance="?android:attr/textAppearanceMedium"
        android:text="NFC Message to be sent"
        android:id="@+id/messageToBeam"
        android:layout_below="@+id/switchOnBtn"
        android:layout_centerHorizontal="true"
        android:layout_marginTop="93dp" />

</RelativeLayout>
```

At this point, we should have something that looks as follows:

Coding the app's internals

We will then move on to the `MainScreen.java` file, which is available at `app` > `src` > `main` > `java` > `package name` > `NFCActivity.java`.

We will implement the project step by step within our code. Don't worry about importing the right statements for our project, as Android Studio will automatically import all the statements that we will need for our project if you have the **Auto-Import** function switched on. If not, please follow the instructions present in the Android section of this chapter.

Feel free to follow along the project through the GitHub Repository where all the source code is available for the readers of our book in its entirety. The repository for this chapter is available at `https://github.com/marcoschwartz/arduino-android-blueprints/tree/master/chapter8/ArduinoNFC`.

We will first start off by declaring the user interface's variables and the necessary variables to get the NFC up and running:

```
    //Declaring the User Interface Variables for mStatusText as a
TextView
    private TextView mStatusText;
    private TextView messageToBeam;
    private Button switchOn;
    private Button switchOff;

    //Initializing the NFC Adapater for sending messages
    NfcAdapter mNfcAdapter;
    private static final int BEAM_BEAMED = 0x1001;
    public static final String MIMETYPE = "application/com.
arduinoandroid.arduinonfc";

    //Keys for Opening and Closing the Relay
    String open_key = "oWnHV6uXre";
    String close_key = "C19HNuqNU4";

    //Getting the name for Log Tags
    private final String TAG = NFCActivity.class.getSimpleName();
```

Within the `onCreate` method, we will implement a number of anonymous classes that we will go through step by step.

In the first part, we will connect the user interface elements to the main Android code:

```
        mStatusText = (TextView) findViewById(R.id.nfcTextStatus);
        messageToBeam = (TextView) findViewById(R.id.messageToBeam);
        switchOn = (Button) findViewById(R.id.switchOnBtn);
        switchOff = (Button) findViewById(R.id.switchOffBtn);
```

Then, in the following code, we need to set `onClickListeners` to our button to be able to change the `TextView` part to the right text to beam the message to our NFC shield. The term *beam* is used in this code section since **Android Beam** is the feature of the Android mobile operating system that allows data to be transferred via NFC.

```
// Adding OnClick Listeners to the Buttons
        switchOn.setOnClickListener(new View.OnClickListener() {
            @Override
            public void onClick(View view) {
                messageToBeam.setText(open_key);
            }
        });
```

```
        switchOff.setOnClickListener(new View.OnClickListener() {
            @Override
            public void onClick(View view) {
                messageToBeam.setText(close_key);
            }
        });
```

In order to enhance the user experience, we need to send a message to the users that they are unable to use this Android application as they don't have NFC enabled on their device:

```
// Check for available NFC Adapter
        mNfcAdapter = NfcAdapter.getDefaultAdapter(this);
        if (mNfcAdapter == null) {
            mStatusText.setText("NFC is not available on this
device.");
        }
```

In the `onCreate()` method, we will also implement our basic NFC callback functions to be able to send and receive a message via NFC:

```
// Register to create and NDEF message when another device is in range
        mNfcAdapter.setNdefPushMessageCallback(new NfcAdapter.
CreateNdefMessageCallback() {
            @Override
            public NdefMessage createNdefMessage(NfcEvent event) {
                //the variable message is from the EditText field
                String message = messageToBeam.getText().toString();
                String text = (message);
                byte[] mime = MIMETYPE.getBytes(Charset.forName("US-
ASCII"));
                NdefRecord mimeMessage = new NdefRecord(
                        NdefRecord.TNF_MIME_MEDIA, mime, new byte[0],
text
                        .getBytes());
                NdefMessage msg = new NdefMessage(
                        new NdefRecord[]{
                                mimeMessage,
                                NdefRecord
                                        .createApplicationRecord("com.
arduinoandroid.arduinonfc")});
                return msg;
            }
        }, this);
```

```
        // And handle the send status
        mNfcAdapter.setOnNdefPushCompleteCallback(
                new NfcAdapter.OnNdefPushCompleteCallback() {

                    @Override
                    public void onNdefPushComplete(NfcEvent event) {
                        mHandler.obtainMessage(BEAM_BEAMED).
sendToTarget();
                    }
                }, this);
```

We need to also implement a method known as `Handler`, which will notify the user via the NFC status text view as to whether the message has been beamed or not:

```
    @SuppressLint("HandlerLeak")
    private final Handler mHandler = new Handler() {
        @Override
        public void handleMessage(Message message) {
            switch (message.what) {
                case BEAM_BEAMED:
                    mStatusText.setText("Your message has been
beamed");
                    break;
            }
        }
    };
```

For the sake of completeness, we will also include the necessary methods to be able to read NDEF messages sent via NFC and to improve app performance by not including a number of different instances within the application:

```
    @Override
    public void onResume() {
        super.onResume();
        // Did we receive an NDEF message?

        Intent intent = getIntent();
        if (NfcAdapter.ACTION_NDEF_DISCOVERED.equals(intent.
getAction())) {
            try {
                Parcelable[] rawMsgs = intent
                        .getParcelableArrayExtra(NfcAdapter.EXTRA_
NDEF_MESSAGES);

                // we created the message, so we know the format
```

```
                NdefMessage msg = (NdefMessage) rawMsgs[0];
                NdefRecord[] records = msg.getRecords();
                byte[] firstPayload = records[0].getPayload();
                String message = new String(firstPayload);
                mStatusText.setText(message);
            } catch (Exception e) {
                Log.e(TAG, "Error retrieving beam message.", e);
            }
        }
    }

    @Override
    public void onNewIntent(Intent intent) {
        setIntent(intent);
    }
```

Once you have included all the methods, you should be able to build the app and run it on your Android physical device with NFC capabilities, running Android 4.3 or higher, and with Android Beam activated within the settings.

You can switch on the relay by tapping the **Switch On** button and, holding the phone against the NFC shield for at least 5 to 10 seconds, and the user interface will get smaller in size. At this point, you need to tap again on the user interface to send your message.

How to go further

This project focused mainly on using NFC to transmit a message and have it read by the Arduino NFC shield.

The ideal user experience would be the user merely tapping the phone against the NFC shield and switching on the light. This could be achieved via **Host-Card Emulation** or with further modification of this baseline project.

Summary

In this chapter, we learned the basic essentials of setting an NFC-enabled Android app. This app communicates with Arduino using the NFC shield and the NFC capabilities of Android 4.3 and higher.

In this, we highlighted the opportunities available for user-engaging projects using NFC. In the next chapter, we will take this to the next level and use Bluetooth to give the user the opportunity to control and engage with a robot.

9
Bluetooth Low Energy Mobile Robot

In this chapter, we are going to use most of the concepts we have learned throughout the book to control a mobile robot via an Android app. The robot will have two motors that we can control, and also an ultrasonic sensor in the front so that it can detect obstacles. The robot will also have a BLE chip so that it can receive commands from the Android app.

The application will have the following basic commands that you will need to control the robot:

- Go forward
- Go backward
- Turn left
- Turn right
- Display the connection status to the robot

The following will be the major takeaways from this chapter:

- Building a mobile robot based on the Arduino platform
- Connecting a BLE module to the Arduino robot
- Building an Android application to control the robot remotely

Hardware and software requirements

Let's first see what we need for this project.

The base of this project is of course the robot itself. For this project, we used a DFRobot miniQ two-wheeled robot chassis. It comes with a round robot chassis, two DC motors, two wheels, and some screws and bolts so that you can mount multiple Arduino boards on it. You can basically use any equivalent robot chassis that has two wheels coupled with DC motors and on which you can mount Arduino-compatible boards.

To control the robot, we are actually going to use three different Arduino boards. The "brain" of the robot will be a simple Arduino Uno board. On top of that, we will use a DFRobot motor shield to control the two DC motors of the robot. And on top of these two boards, we will put a prototyping shield so that we can connect different modules to the robot.

To control the robot remotely, we will again use BLE. To give BLE connectivity to the robot, we used an Adafruit nRF8001 breakout board.

To give the robot the ability to detect what is in front of it, we added an URM37 ultrasonic sensor to the project. As we will see, this sensor is really easy to interface with Arduino.

Finally, you will also need some jumper wires to make the different connections between the robot, the sensor, and the Bluetooth module.

The following is a list of all of the hardware you will need for this project, along with links to these parts on the web:

- An Arduino Uno board (`http://www.dfrobot.com/index.php?route=product/product&search=uno&description=true&product_id=838`)
- An Arduino motor shield (`http://www.dfrobot.com/index.php?route=product/product&path=35_39&product_id=59`)
- An Arduino prototyping shield (`http://www.dfrobot.com/index.php?route=product/product&product_id=55`)
- An nRF8001 breakout board (`https://www.adafruit.com/products/1697`)
- An ultrasonic range sensor (`http://www.dfrobot.com/index.php?route=product/product&search=ultrasonic&description=true&page=1&product_id=53`)

- An ultrasonic sensor mounting kit (`http://www.dfrobot.com/index.php?route=product/product&product_id=322`)
- A DFRobot miniQ chassis (`http://www.dfrobot.com/index.php?route=product/product&search=miniq&description=true&product_id=367`)
- A 7.4 V battery (`http://www.dfrobot.com/index.php?route=product/product&product_id=489`)
- Jumper wires (`https://www.adafruit.com/products/1957`)

On the software side, you will of course need the Arduino IDE. You will also need the following:

- A library for the nRF8001 chip (`https://github.com/adafruit/Adafruit_nRF8001`)
- The aREST library to send commands to the robot (`https://github.com/marcoschwartz/aREST`)

Configuring the hardware

We are first going to assemble the robot itself, and then see how to connect the Bluetooth module and the ultrasonic sensor. To give you an idea of what you should end up with, the following is a front-view image of the robot when fully assembled:

The following image shows the back of the robot when fully assembled:

The first step is to assemble the robot chassis. To do so, you can watch the DFRobot assembly guide at `https://www.youtube.com/watch?v=tKakeyL_8Fg`.

Then, you need to attach the different Arduino boards and shields to the robot. Use the spacers found in the robot chassis kit to mount the Arduino Uno board first. Then put the Arduino motor shield on top of that. At this point, use the screw header terminals to connect the two DC motors to the motor shield. This is how it should look at this point:

Finally, mount the prototyping shield on top of the motor shield.

We are now going to connect the BLE module and the ultrasonic sensor to the Arduino prototyping shield. The following is a schematic diagram showing the connections between the Arduino Uno board (done via the prototyping shield in our case) and the components:

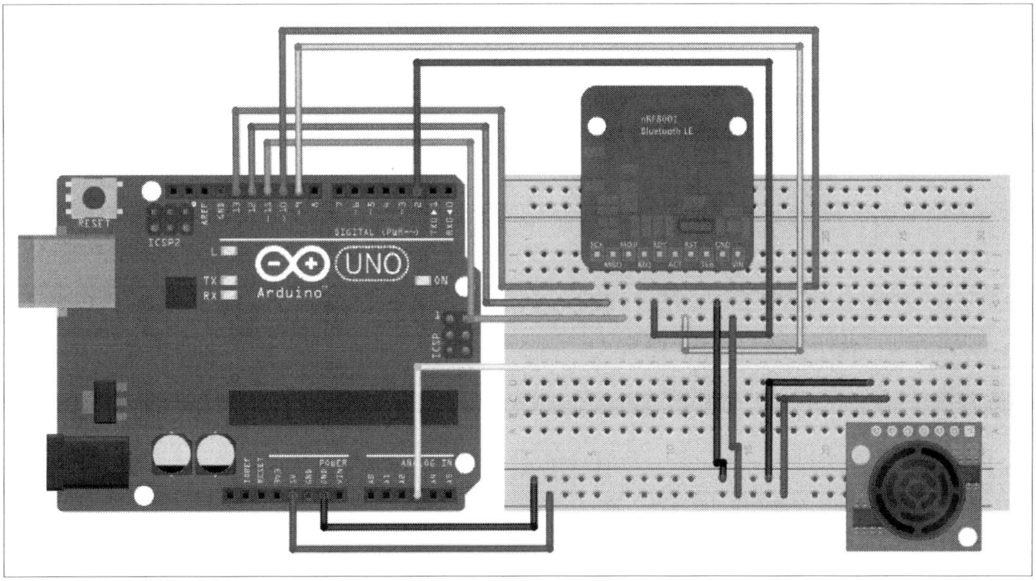

Now perform the following steps:

1. First, we are now going to connect the BLE module.
2. Place the module on the prototyping shield.
3. Connect the power supply of the module as follows: **GND** goes to the prototyping shield's **GND** pin, and **VIN** goes to the prototyping shield's +5V.
4. After that, you need to connect the different wires responsible for the SPI interface: **SCK** to Arduino pin **13**, **MISO** to Arduino pin **12**, and **MOSI** to Arduino pin **11**.
5. Then connect the **REQ** pin to Arduino pin **10**.
6. Finally, connect the **RDY** pin to Arduino pin **2** and the **RST** pin to Arduino pin **9**.

7. For the URM37 module, connect the **VCC** pin of the module to Arduino +5V, **GND** to **GND**, and the **PWM** pin to the Arduino **A3** pin.

> To review the pin order on the URM37 module, you can check the official DFRobot documentation at `http://www.dfrobot.com/wiki/index.php?title=URM37_V3.2_Ultrasonic_Sensor_(SKU:SEN0001)`.

The following is a close-up image of the prototyping shield with the BLE module connected:

8. Finally, connect the 7.4 V battery to the Arduino Uno board power jack. The battery is simply placed below the Arduino Uno board.

Testing the robot

We are now going to write a sketch to test the different functionalities of the robot, first without using Bluetooth. As the sketch is quite long, we will look at the code piece by piece. Before you proceed, make sure that the battery is always plugged into the robot. Now perform the following steps:

1. The sketch starts by including the aREST library that we will use to control the robot via serial commands:

```
#include <aREST.h>
```

2. Now we declare which pins the motors are connected to:

```
int speed_motor1 = 6;
int speed_motor2 = 5;
int direction_motor1 = 7;
int direction_motor2 = 4;
```

3. We also declare which pin the ultrasonic sensor is connected to:

```
int distance_sensor = A3;
```

4. Then, we create an instance of the aREST library:

```
aREST rest = aREST();
```

5. To store the distance data measured by the ultrasonic sensor, we declare a distance variable:

```
int distance;
```

6. In the `setup()` function of the sketch, we first initialize serial communications that we will use to communicate with the robot for this test:

```
Serial.begin(115200);
```

7. We also expose the distance variable to the REST API, so we can access it easily:

```
rest.variable("distance",&distance);
```

8. To control the robot, we are going to declare a whole set of functions that will perform the basic operations: going forward, going backward, turning on itself (left or right), and stopping. We will see the details of these functions in a moment; for now, we just need to expose them to the API:

```
rest.function("forward",forward);
rest.function("backward",backward);
rest.function("left",left);
rest.function("right",right);
rest.function("stop",stop);
```

9. We also give the robot an ID and a name:

```
rest.set_id("001");
rest.set_name("mobile_robot");
```

10. In the `loop()` function of the sketch, we first measure the distance from the sensor:

```
distance = measure_distance(distance_sensor);
```

11. We then handle the requests using the aREST library:

```
rest.handle(Serial);
```

12. Now, we will look at the functions for controlling the motors. They are all based on a function to control a single motor, where we need to set the motor pins, the speed, and the direction of the motor:

```
void send_motor_command(int speed_pin, int direction_pin, int pwm,
boolean dir)
{
  analogWrite(speed_pin, pwm); // Set PWM control, 0 for stop, and
255 for maximum speed
  digitalWrite(direction_pin, dir); // Dir set the rotation
direction of the motor (true or false means forward or reverse)
}
```

13. Based on this function, we can now define the different functions to move the robot, such as `forward`:

```
int forward(String command) {

  send_motor_command(speed_motor1,direction_motor1,100,1);
  send_motor_command(speed_motor2,direction_motor2,100,1);
  return 1;
}
```

14. We also define a `backward` function, simply inverting the direction of both motors:

```
int backward(String command) {
  send_motor_command(speed_motor1,direction_motor1,100,0);
  send_motor_command(speed_motor2,direction_motor2,100,0);
  return 1;
}
```

15. To make the robot turn left, we simply make the motors rotate in opposite directions:

```
int left(String command) {
  send_motor_command(speed_motor1,direction_motor1,75,0);
  send_motor_command(speed_motor2,direction_motor2,75,1);
  return 1;
}
```

16. We also have a function to stop the robot:

```
int stop(String command) {
  send_motor_command(speed_motor1,direction_motor1,0,1);
  send_motor_command(speed_motor2,direction_motor2,0,1);
  return 1;
}
```

There is also a function to make the robot turn right, which is not detailed here. Note that all of the code used in this chapter can be found in the GitHub repository of the book at `https://github.com/marcoschwartz/arduino-android-blueprints`.

We are now going to test the robot. Before you do anything, ensure that the battery is always plugged into the robot. This will ensure that the motors are not trying to get power from your computer USB port, which could damage it.

Also place some small support at the bottom of the robot so that the wheels don't touch the ground. This will ensure that you can test all the commands of the robot without the robot moving too far from your computer, as it is still attached via the USB cable.

Now you can upload the sketch to your Arduino Uno board. Open the serial monitor and type the following:

```
/forward
```

This should make both the wheels of the robot turn in the same direction. You can also try the other commands to move the robot to make sure they all work properly. Then, test the ultrasonic distance sensor by typing the following:

```
/distance
```

You should get back the distance (in centimeters) in front of the sensor:

```
{"distance": 24, "id": "001", "name": "mobile_robot", "connected": true}
```

Try changing the distance by putting your hand in front of the sensor and typing the command again.

Writing the Arduino sketch

Now that we have made sure that the robot is working properly, we can write the final sketch that will receive the commands via Bluetooth. As the sketch shares many similarities with the test sketch, we are only going to see what is added compared to the test sketch. We first need to include more libraries:

```
#include <SPI.h>
#include "Adafruit_BLE_UART.h"
#include <aREST.h>
```

We also define which pins the BLE module is connected to:

```
#define ADAFRUITBLE_REQ 10
#define ADAFRUITBLE_RDY 2     // This should be an interrupt pin, on
Uno thats #2 or #3
#define ADAFRUITBLE_RST 9
```

We have to create an instance of the BLE module:

```
Adafruit_BLE_UART BTLEserial = Adafruit_BLE_UART(ADAFRUITBLE_REQ,
ADAFRUITBLE_RDY, ADAFRUITBLE_RST);
```

In the `setup()` function of the sketch, we initialize the BLE chip:

```
BTLEserial.begin();
```

In the `loop()` function, we check the status of the BLE chip and store it in a variable:

```
BTLEserial.pollACI();
aci_evt_opcode_t status = BTLEserial.getState();
```

If we detect that a device is connected to the chip, we handle the incoming request with the aREST library, which will allow us to use the same commands as before to control the robot:

```
if (status == ACI_EVT_CONNECTED) {
  rest.handle(BTLEserial);
}
```

You can now upload the code to your Arduino board, again by making sure that the battery is connected to the Arduino Uno board via the power jack. You can now move on to the development of the Android application to control the robot.

Setting up the Android app

The Android application that we will be creating will give us the opportunity to control the robot via BLE from the physical Android device. This application will have five basic controls, that is, **Forward**, **Backward**, **Left**, **Right**, and **Stop**. In addition, it will also show the BLE connection status and there will be a **Refresh** button that will allow us to refresh the Bluetooth callback.

We will assume that you will have switched on the `Auto-Import` function within your preferences. If not, activate it by going to the **Auto-Import** preferences and selecting all the available options. The **Auto-Import** preferences are available on Mac and Windows as follows:

- On a Mac, navigate to **Android Studio** > **Preferences** > **Editor** > **Auto-Import**
- On Windows, navigate to **File** > **Settings** > **Editor** > **Auto-Import**

With all the necessary settings in place, we will start off by creating a new project where we will choose the following within the **New Project** setup walkthrough:

- **Name**: `Mobile Robot`
- **Minimum SDK**: `18`
- **Project**: `Blank Activity`
- **Activity Name**: `RobotControlActivity`
- **Domain**: `arduinoandroid.com`

Laying out the Android user interface and setting permissions

In order to make this project work, we will need to first go over to the Android `Manifest` file, which is available at `app` > `src` > `main` > `AndroidManifest.xml`.

Since this Android application uses BLE to connect the Android physical device to the robot, we will need to add the following permissions to the Android `Manifest` file. These permissions will allow the application to connect to the paired Bluetooth devices that have been discovered:

```
<uses-permission android:name="android.permission.BLUETOOTH"/>
<uses-permission android:name="android.permission.BLUETOOTH_ADMIN"/>
```

The next step that we will take is to set up the very basic Android layout file so that we can implement the app's functions and allow the user to activate the voice recognition intent.

In our project, we will navigate to the main layout file which can be accessed from `app` > `src` > `res` > `layout` > `activity_robot_control.xml`.

There are a number of layout formats with the Android user interface design, and in this particular case, we will be using a horizontal linear layout with a vertical linear layout as a child. Keeping these concepts in mind, we will replace the current code with the following lines of code:

```
<LinearLayout
    android:orientation="vertical"
    android:layout_width="fill_parent"
    android:layout_height="fill_parent"
    xmlns:android="http://schemas.android.com/apk/res/android">

    <Button
        android:layout_width="wrap_content"
        android:layout_height="wrap_content"
```

```
        android:text="Connect"
        android:id="@+id/connectBtn"
        android:layout_gravity="center_horizontal"
        />

    <Button
        style="?android:attr/buttonStyleSmall"
        android:layout_width="wrap_content"
        android:layout_height="wrap_content"
        android:text="Forward"
        android:id="@+id/fwdBtn"
        android:layout_gravity="center_horizontal"
        />

    <LinearLayout
        android:orientation="horizontal"
        android:layout_width="fill_parent"
        android:layout_height="57dp">

        <Button
            style="?android:attr/buttonStyleSmall"
            android:layout_width="wrap_content"
            android:layout_height="wrap_content"
            android:text="Left"
            android:id="@+id/leftBtn"
            android:layout_weight="1"
            />

        <Button
            android:layout_width="wrap_content"
            android:layout_height="wrap_content"
            android:text="Stop"
            android:id="@+id/stopBtn"
            android:layout_gravity="center_horizontal"
            android:layout_weight="1"
            />

        <Button
            style="?android:attr/buttonStyleSmall"
            android:layout_width="wrap_content"
            android:layout_height="wrap_content"
            android:text="Right"
            android:id="@+id/rightBtn"
            android:layout_weight="1"
            />
```

```
        </LinearLayout>

        <Button
            android:layout_width="wrap_content"
            android:layout_height="wrap_content"
            android:text="Backward"
            android:id="@+id/backwardBtn"
            android:layout_gravity="center_horizontal"
            />

        <TextView
            android:layout_width="wrap_content"
            android:layout_height="wrap_content"
            android:text="Connection Status View"
            android:id="@+id/connectionStsView"
            android:layout_gravity="center_horizontal"
            />

    </LinearLayout>
```

At this point, you should end up with something that looks like the following screenshot. This is based on the LG Nexus 5:

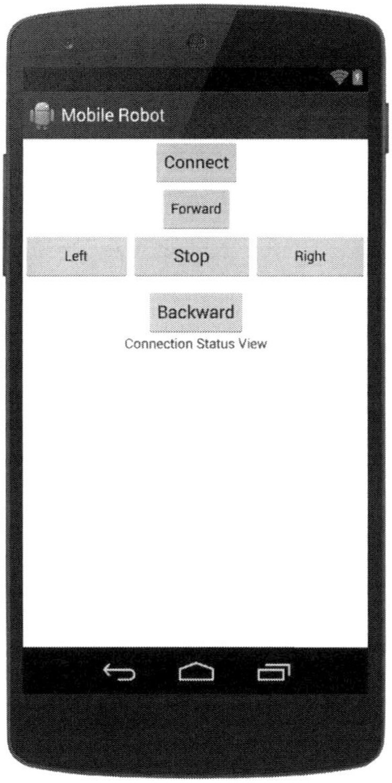

Coding the app's internals

At this point, we want to start connecting our freshly designed Android user interface to the main Android code, and we will start doing this by opening the `RobotControlActivity.java` file, which is available at `app` > `src` > `main` > `java` > `package name` > `RobotControlActivity.java`.

We will start off by declaring the user interface element variables together with the main variable, which we could use for logging, as follows:

```
//User Interface Elements
    Button fwdBtn;
    Button leftBtn;
    Button rightBtn;
    Button backBtn;
    Button stopBtn;
    Button connectBtn;
    TextView connectionSts;

    //Logging Variables
    private final String LOG_TAG = RobotControlActivity.class.
getSimpleName();
```

We will declare all the necessary variables for the `BluetoothCallback` variable, where we will primarily declare the UUIDs associated with our specific BLE module, followed by the Bluetooth adapter variables and characteristics:

```
    // UUIDs for UAT service and associated characteristics.
    public static UUID UART_UUID = UUID.fromString("6E400001-B5A3-
F393-E0A9-E50E24DCCA9E");
    public static UUID TX_UUID = UUID.fromString("6E400002-B5A3-F393-
E0A9-E50E24DCCA9E");
    public static UUID RX_UUID = UUID.fromString("6E400003-B5A3-F393-
E0A9-E50E24DCCA9E");

    // UUID for the BTLE client characteristic which is necessary for
notifications.
    public static UUID CLIENT_UUID = UUID.fromString("00002902-0000-
1000-8000-00805f9b34fb");

    // BTLE states
    private BluetoothAdapter adapter;
    private BluetoothGatt gatt;
    private BluetoothGattCharacteristic tx;
    private BluetoothGattCharacteristic rx;
```

We will then proceed to the `onCreate()` method and connect the different user interface elements to the code:

```
        fwdBtn = (Button) findViewById(R.id.fwdBtn);
        leftBtn = (Button) findViewById(R.id.leftBtn);
        rightBtn = (Button) findViewById(R.id.rightBtn);
        backBtn = (Button) findViewById(R.id.backwardBtn);
        stopBtn = (Button) findViewById(R.id.stopBtn);
        connectBtn = (Button) findViewById(R.id.connectBtn);

        connectionSts = (TextView)findViewById(R.
id.connectionStsView);
```

In this project, we would like to send specific BLE messages to our robot when the user taps on the buttons, and in this part, we will be adding `onClickListeners` to our buttons which we have connected earlier to send the messages that we need to interface with the robot:

```
fwdBtn.setOnClickListener(new View.OnClickListener() {
            @Override
            public void onClick(View view) {
                String setOutputMessage = "/forward /";
                tx.setValue(setOutputMessage.getBytes(Charset.
forName("UTF-8")));
                if (gatt.writeCharacteristic(tx)) {
                    writeConnectionData("Sent: " + setOutputMessage);
                } else {
                    writeConnectionData("Couldn't write TX
characteristic!");
                }
            }
        });

        leftBtn.setOnClickListener(new View.OnClickListener() {
            @Override
            public void onClick(View view) {
                String setOutputMessage = "/left /";
                tx.setValue(setOutputMessage.getBytes(Charset.
forName("UTF-8")));
                if (gatt.writeCharacteristic(tx)) {
                    writeConnectionData("Sent: " + setOutputMessage);
                } else {
                    writeConnectionData("Couldn't write TX
characteristic!");
                }
```

```
            }
        });

        rightBtn.setOnClickListener(new View.OnClickListener() {
            @Override
            public void onClick(View view) {
                String setOutputMessage = "/right /";
                tx.setValue(setOutputMessage.getBytes(Charset.
forName("UTF-8")));
                if (gatt.writeCharacteristic(tx)) {
                    writeConnectionData("Sent: " + setOutputMessage);
                } else {
                    writeConnectionData("Couldn't write TX
characteristic!");
                }
            }
        });
        backBtn.setOnClickListener(new View.OnClickListener() {
            @Override
            public void onClick(View view) {
                String setOutputMessage = "/backward /";
                tx.setValue(setOutputMessage.getBytes(Charset.
forName("UTF-8")));
                if (gatt.writeCharacteristic(tx)) {
                    writeConnectionData("Sent: " + setOutputMessage);
                } else {
                    writeConnectionData("Couldn't write TX
characteristic!");
                }
            }
        });
        stopBtn.setOnClickListener(new View.OnClickListener() {
            @Override
            public void onClick(View view) {
                String setOutputMessage = "/stop /";
                tx.setValue(setOutputMessage.getBytes(Charset.
forName("UTF-8")));
                if (gatt.writeCharacteristic(tx)) {
                    writeConnectionData("Sent: " + setOutputMessage);
                } else {
                    writeConnectionData("Couldn't write TX
characteristic!");
                }
            }
        });
```

```
        connectBtn.setOnClickListener(new View.OnClickListener() {
            @Override
            public void onClick(View view) {

                restartScan();
            }
        });
```

In the next section, we need to declare a new method, which we will name `writeConnectionData`. Its main role is writing the status of the Bluetooth callback to the connection status text view:

```
private void writeConnectionData(final CharSequence text) {
        Log.e(LOG_TAG, text.toString());
        connectionSts.setText(text.toString());
    }
```

The following code is all the necessary Bluetooth callback which needs to take place in order to establish a connection between the Android physical device and BLE module on the robot:

```
private BluetoothGattCallback bluetoothGattCallback = new
BluetoothGattCallback() {
        // Called whenever the device connection state changes, i.e.
from disconnected to connected.
        @Override
        public void onConnectionStateChange(BluetoothGatt gatt, int
status, int newState) {
            super.onConnectionStateChange(gatt, status, newState);
            if (newState == BluetoothGatt.STATE_CONNECTED) {
                writeConnectionData("Connected!");
                // Discover services.
                if (!gatt.discoverServices()) {
                    writeConnectionData("Failed to start discovering
services!");
                }
            } else if (newState == BluetoothGatt.STATE_DISCONNECTED) {
                writeConnectionData("Disconnected!");
            } else {
                writeConnectionData("Connection state changed.  New
state: " + newState);
            }
        }
```

```
        // Called when services have been discovered on the remote
device.
        // It seems to be necessary to wait for this discovery to
occur before
        // manipulating any services or characteristics.
        public void onServicesDiscovered(BluetoothGatt gatt, int
status) {
            super.onServicesDiscovered(gatt, status);
            if (status == BluetoothGatt.GATT_SUCCESS) {
                writeConnectionData("Service discovery completed!");
            } else {
                writeConnectionData("Service discovery failed with
status: " + status);
            }
            // Save reference to each characteristic.
            tx = gatt.getService(UART_UUID).getCharacteristic(TX_
UUID);
            rx = gatt.getService(UART_UUID).getCharacteristic(RX_
UUID);

            // Setup notifications on RX characteristic changes (i.e.
data received).
            // First call setCharacteristicNotification to enable
notification.
            if (!gatt.setCharacteristicNotification(rx, true)) {
                writeConnectionData("Couldn't set notifications for RX
characteristic!");
            }

            // Next update the RX characteristic's client descriptor
to enable notifications.
            if (rx.getDescriptor(CLIENT_UUID) != null) {
                BluetoothGattDescriptor desc =
rx.getDescriptor(CLIENT_UUID);
                desc.setValue(BluetoothGattDescriptor.ENABLE_
NOTIFICATION_VALUE);
                if (!gatt.writeDescriptor(desc)) {
                    writeConnectionData("Couldn't write RX client
descriptor value!");
                }
            } else {
                writeConnectionData("Couldn't get RX client
descriptor!");
            }
            areServicesAccessible = true;
        }
    };
```

The Android application's life cycle gives us the ability to add methods that can be activated at different parts of this cycle. The following `onStart()` and `onStop()` methods, which are invoked on starting and exiting the application respectively, allow us to conserve the device's energy and memory resources:

```
protected void onStart() {
        Log.d(LOG_TAG,"onStart has been called");
        super.onStart();
        // / Scan for all BTLE devices.
        // The first one with the UART service will be chosen--see the
code in the scanCallback.
        adapter = BluetoothAdapter.getDefaultAdapter();
        startScan();
    }

    //When this Activity isn't visible anymore
    protected void onStop() {
        Log.d(LOG_TAG,"onStop has been called");
        //disconnect and close Bluetooth Connection for better
reliability
        if (gatt != null) {
            gatt.disconnect();
            gatt.close();
            gatt = null;
            tx = null;
            rx = null;
        }
        super.onStop();
    }
```

In order to allow the starting, stopping, and restarting of Bluetooth scans, we need to declare methods to do these particular actions, which is the purpose of the following code:

```
private void startScan() {
        if (!adapter.isEnabled()) {
            adapter.enable();
        }
        if (!adapter.isDiscovering()) {
            adapter.startDiscovery();
        }
        writeConnectionData("Scanning for devices...");
        adapter.startLeScan(scanCallback);
    }
```

```
    private void stopScan() {
        if (adapter.isDiscovering()) {
            adapter.cancelDiscovery();
        }
        writeConnectionData("Stopping scan");
        adapter.stopLeScan(scanCallback);
    }

    private void restartScan() {
        stopScan();
        startScan();
    }
```

The most important part of the Bluetooth callback is to connect to the right BLE device, and the following code helps the user to achieve that:

```
private BluetoothAdapter.LeScanCallback scanCallback = new
BluetoothAdapter.LeScanCallback() {
        // Called when a device is found.
        @Override
        public void onLeScan(BluetoothDevice bluetoothDevice, int i,
byte[] bytes) {
            Log.d(LOG_TAG, bluetoothDevice.getAddress());

            writeConnectionData("Found device: " + bluetoothDevice.
getAddress());

            // Check if the device has the UART service.
            if (BluetoothUtils.parseUUIDs(bytes).contains(UART_UUID))
{
                // Found a device, stop the scan.
                adapter.stopLeScan(scanCallback);
                writeConnectionData("Found UART service!");
                // Connect to the device.
                // Control flow will now go to the
bluetoothGattCallback functions when BTLE events occur.
                gatt = bluetoothDevice.connectGatt(getApplicationConte
xt(), false, bluetoothGattCallback);
            }
        }
    };
```

UUID parsing, unlike in the previous chapters, has been moved to a `utility` class in order to refactor the code and make it more readable. In order to create a `utility` class, we first need to right-click on our package name and create a new package called `Bluetooth`.

After that, we will right-click on the new package, select **New** > **Java Class**, and name the new class as `BluetoothUtils`.

After the preceding two steps, we will replace the code within the class with the following code:

```
public class BluetoothUtils {

    // Filtering by custom UUID is broken in Android 4.3 and 4.4, see:
    //   http://stackoverflow.com/questions/18019161/startlescan-with-
128-bit-uuids-doesnt-work-on-native-android-ble-implementation?noredir
ect=1#comment27879874_18019161
    // This is a workaround function from the SO thread to manually
parse advertisement data.
    public static List<UUID> parseUUIDs(final byte[] advertisedData) {
        List<UUID> uuids = new ArrayList<UUID>();

        int offset = 0;
        while (offset < (advertisedData.length - 2)) {
            int len = advertisedData[offset++];
            if (len == 0)
                break;

            int type = advertisedData[offset++];
            switch (type) {
                case 0x02: // Partial list of 16-bit UUIDs
                case 0x03: // Complete list of 16-bit UUIDs
                    while (len > 1) {
                        int uuid16 = advertisedData[offset++];
                        uuid16 += (advertisedData[offset++] << 8);
                        len -= 2;
                        uuids.add(UUID.fromString(String.format("%08x-
0000-1000-8000-00805f9b34fb", uuid16)));
                    }
                    break;
                case 0x06:// Partial list of 128-bit UUIDs
                case 0x07:// Complete list of 128-bit UUIDs
                    // Loop through the advertised 128-bit UUID's.
                    while (len >= 16) {
                        try {
                            // Wrap the advertised bits and order
them.
                            ByteBuffer buffer = ByteBuffer.
wrap(advertisedData, offset++, 16).order(ByteOrder.LITTLE_ENDIAN);
```

```
                                    long mostSignificantBit = buffer.
getLong();
                                    long leastSignificantBit = buffer.
getLong();
                                    uuids.add(new UUID(leastSignificantBit,
                                            mostSignificantBit));
                                } catch (IndexOutOfBoundsException e) {
                                    // Defensive programming.
                                    //Log.e(LOG_TAG, e.toString());
                                    continue;
                                } finally {
                                    // Move the offset to read the next uuid.
                                    offset += 15;
                                    len -= 16;
                                }
                            }
                            break;
                        default:
                            offset += (len - 1);
                            break;
                    }
                }
                return uuids;
            }
        }
```

At this point, you could go ahead, build, and run the project on an Android physical device running Android 4.3 with Bluetooth switched on.

Enhancing the user interface further

Once we have managed to finalize our code and assure ourselves that the user interface includes all the basic functionalities required to control the robot, we can proceed to improving our user interface.

We will improve the user interface with two main actions:

- Adding a new app icon
- Styling the user interface buttons

Adding a new app icon

First, we will download the image asset. It's available within the GitHub repository and also as a public download at `http://bit.ly/mobileroboticon`.

You should navigate to the project tree, followed by a right-click on **app**.

When you right-click on **app**, create a new image asset by going to **New** > **Image Asset**.

You will then be shown an **Asset Studio** pop-up window, which will allow you to choose your very own image file. For optimization purposes, we recommend that you go for a `.png` file with a resolution of 144 pixels by 144 pixels. Android Studio automatically does all the resizing and resource creation to adapt your graphic to different screens.

Once you choose the `ic_launcher` image file that we have provided you with, you will be shown a screen with the icon in different sizes. Click on **Next** where you will see the screen with the launcher icons in different sizes.

This screen warns you that previous files will be overwritten and shows you the image launcher file in a number of different resolutions once again. Click on **Finish.** Then compile the app, launch it on your physical device, and you should see something pleasant in your app tray and in the app's action bar.

Styling the user interface buttons

The final steps that we will be taking about are to modify our buttons and add some color to the text.

There are two steps required while creating the new buttons:

1. Create a `Drawable` folder with a new XML drawable file known as `button.xml`.
2. Then connect the drawable resource file to the main Android layout file.

Create the `Drawable` folder by right-clicking on the `res` folder, which is available at `App` > `src` > `main` > `res`.

After creating the `Drawable` folder within the `res` folder, we need to once again right-click on the new `drawable` folder and navigate to **New** > **Drawable Resource File**.

Name the file `buttonshape` and type `shape` as the root element, followed by clicking on **OK**.

Within the `button.xml` file, replace the current code with the following:

```
<shape xmlns:android="http://schemas.android.com/apk/res/android">
    <corners
        android:radius="30dp"/>
    <solid
        android:color="#FFFFFF"/>
    <padding
        android:left="10dp"
        android:top="10dp"
        android:right="10dp"
        android:bottom="10dp"/>
    <stroke
        android:width="2dp"
        android:color="#4A90E2"/>
</shape>
```

At this point, the buttons have not been modified yet, so we will go to the robot control activity layout file, which is available at `app` > `main` > `res` > `layout` > `activity_robot_control.xml`.

Within this file, we will also be connecting the changes within the `buttonshape.xml` file to the main layout file, and we will be adding `margin` to the buttons so that there is enough spacing between the buttons for a presentable layout.

We will add the following code to all the button elements to give them the `buttonshape` styling:

```
android:background="@drawable/buttonshape"
```

After that, we will add the margins by adding the following code to the **Connect**, **Backward**, and **Forward** buttons:

```
android:layout_margin="10dp"
```

For the left and right buttons, we will add the following code since they're within a different kind of layout:

```
android:layout_marginLeft="10dp"
android:layout_marginRight="10dp"
```

At this point, you should have a layout that looks like the following screenshot on Nexus 4, which is more attractive and presentable to the user:

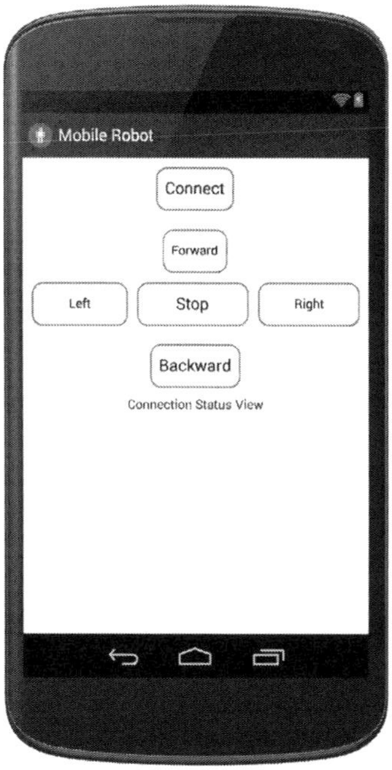

How to go further

The Android application can be further enhanced with more refined controls that could quantify the exact angle by which you would like the robot to turn left or right. We can also extract data from the ultrasonic sensor and display it within the Android application to get data about the proximity to obstacles.

In addition, the Android application will definitely benefit from the addition of a **Connection** dialog that shows the user all the available BLE devices, and the user can choose the BLE Chip connected to the robot. This will enhance user experience and, at the same time, provide a more stable connection with the robot, especially if you're working in an environment surrounded by other BLE transmitters.

Last but not least, the reader can also go ahead and do further modifications to the user interface and layout to make the app even more attractive and presentable. Our main recommendation is to follow the design guidelines available at `http://developer.android.com`.

Summary

In this chapter, we managed to create our very own mobile robot together with a companion Android application that we can use to control our robot.

We achieved this step by step by setting up an Arduino-enabled robot and coding the companion Android application. It uses the BLE software and hardware of an Android physical device running on Android 4.3 or higher.

In the final chapter, we will consider a more direct form of user interaction, by measuring our pulse rate using Android, Arduino, and a specific sensor.

10
Pulse Rate Sensor

In this chapter, we will start exploring the possibilities of using Arduino and Android in a health context. The most natural way to start off such an adventure is to create a project that involves an open source pulse rate sensor. This sensor will be connected to a BLE-equipped Arduino. The data will be displayed in an interesting way within the Android app to make the experience as seamless as possible.

The following will be the major takeaways from this chapter:

- Using a pulse rate sensor with Arduino to measure your heart rate
- Connecting a BLE module to Arduino to transmit pulse rate data
- Visualizing this data in an Android application

Hardware and software requirements

Let's first see what we need for this project. As usual, we will use an Arduino Uno board.

You will also need a heart rate sensor, which is the most important component of this chapter. We used a sensor that is compatible with Arduino, simply called the pulse sensor (`http://pulsesensor.com/`).

The following is an image of the sensor we used:

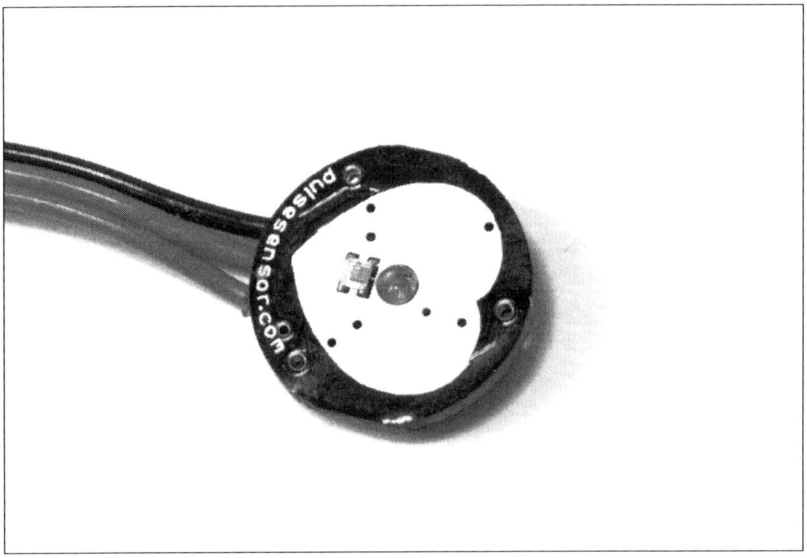

For wireless communications, we used the nRF8001 BLE breakout board that we used in previous chapters.

Finally, you will need a breadboard and some jumper wires to make the connections between the different parts.

This is the list of all of the hardware you will need for this project, along with links to find these parts on the web:

- Arduino Uno board (`https://www.adafruit.com/products/50`)
- nRF8001 breakout board (`https://www.adafruit.com/products/1697`)
- Heart rate sensor (`http://pulsesensor.myshopify.com/products/pulse-sensor-amped`)
- Breadboard (`https://www.adafruit.com/products/64`)
- Jumper wires (`https://www.adafruit.com/products/1957`)

On the software side, you will of course need the Arduino IDE. You will also need the following:

- The library for the nRF8001 chip, available at `https://github.com/adafruit/Adafruit_nRF8001`
- The aREST library to send commands to the robot, available at `https://github.com/marcoschwartz/aREST`

Configuring our hardware

We are now going to build the project by performing the following steps:

1. First, connect the BLE breakout board to the Arduino Uno board.
2. Place the module on the breadboard.
3. Connect the power supply of the module: **GND** goes to prototyping shield **GND** and **VIN** goes to the prototyping shield +5V.
4. Connect the different wires responsible for the SPI interface: **SCK** to Arduino pin **13**, **MISO** to Arduino pin **12**, and **MOSI** to Arduino pin **11**.
5. Then connect the **REQ** pin to Arduino pin 10.
6. Finally, connect the **RDY** pin to Arduino pin **2** and the **RST** pin to Arduino pin **9**.

   The following is a schematic diagram to help you out for this part:

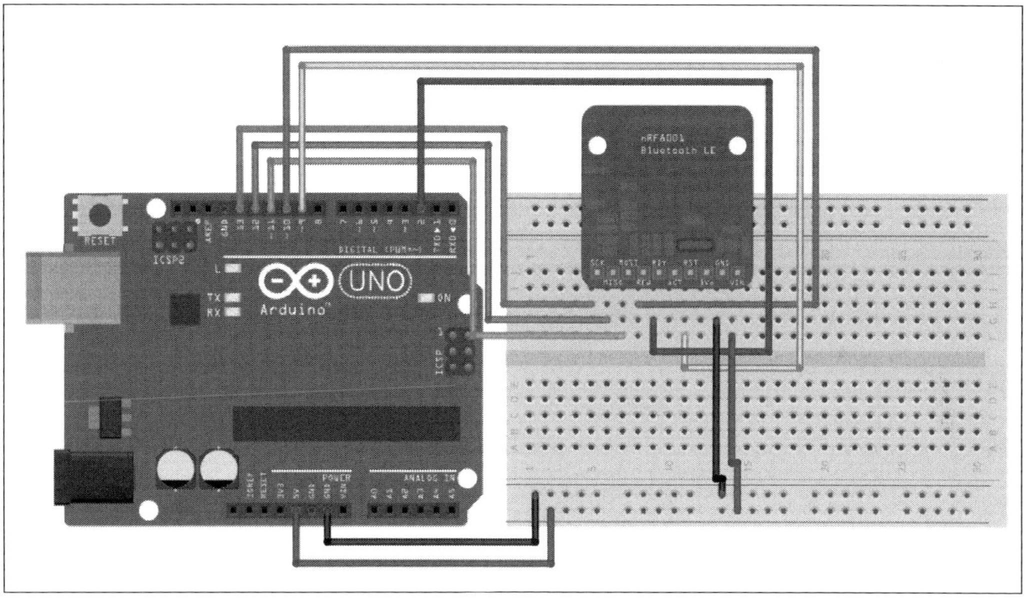

7. Now, connecting the pulse rate sensor is actually very simple. You simply need to connect the red wire to the Arduino +5V pin, the black cable to the Arduino GND pin, and the remaining pin to the Arduino A0 pin.

This is an image of the fully assembled project:

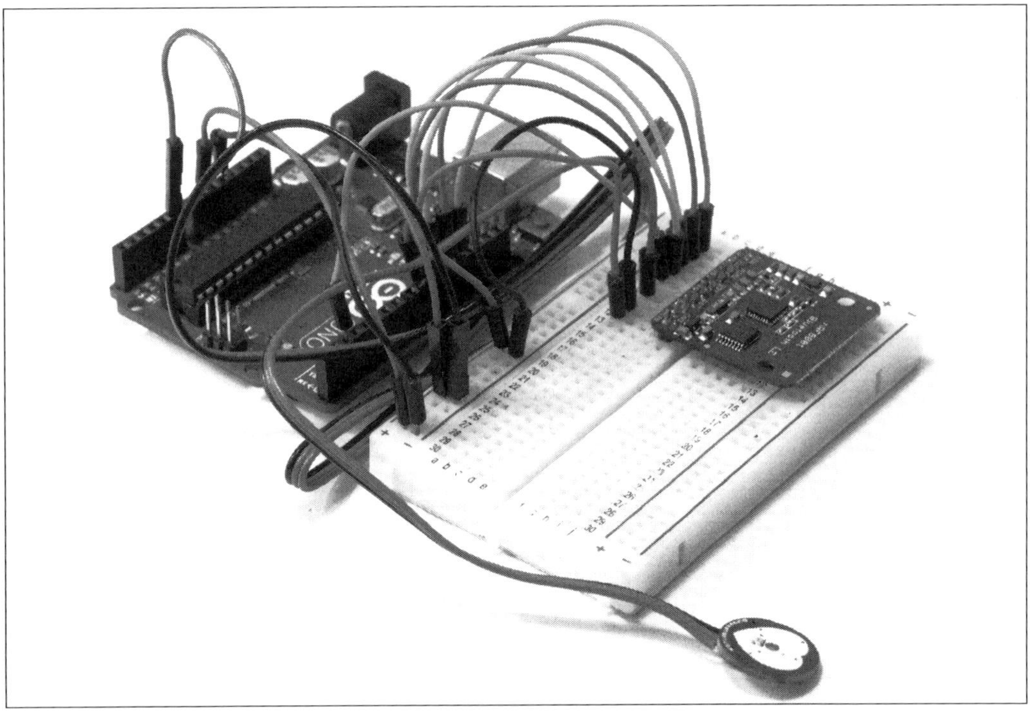

If you want more details about the pulse rate sensor, you can visit the official documentation at `http://pulsesensor.myshopify.com/pages/code-and-guide`.

Testing the sensor

We are now going to write some basic code to make sure that the pulse sensor is correctly wired and that it is not damaged. Thanks to the work done by the creator of the sensor, it is actually very easy to extract the heart pulse rate from the sensor readings. The following sketch starts by defining a lot of variables that are required for the calculation of the **Beats Per Minute** (**BPM**):

```
// Sensor and pins variables
int pulsePin = 0;
int blinkPin = 13;

// Pulse rate variable
volatile int BPM;
```

```
// Raw signal
volatile int Signal;

// Interval between beats
volatile int IBI = 600; // Default Inter Beats Interval

// Becomes true when the pulse is high
volatile boolean Pulse = false;

// Becomes true when Arduino finds a pulse (QS stands for Quantified
Self here)
volatile boolean QS = false;
```

In the `setup()` function of the sketch, we simply start the serial communications and initialize the readings from the pulse sensor:

```
// Start Serial
Serial.begin(115200);

// Sets up to read Pulse Sensor signal every 2mS
interruptSetup();
```

Then, in the `loop()` function of the sketch, we constantly check to see if we found a heart beat, and we print it on the serial monitor if this is the case:

```
  // If heart beat is found
  if (QS == true) {

    // Print heart rate
    Serial.print("Heart rate: ");
    Serial.println(BPM);

    // Reset the Quantified Self flag for next time
    QS = false;
   }

  // Wait 20 ms
  delay(20);
}
```

> Note that all of the code used in this chapter can be found in the GitHub repository of the book at `https://github.com/marcoschwartz/arduino-android-blueprints`.

It is now time to test the code. Before uploading the code to your board, it's recommended that you watch a video found at `http://pulsesensor.myshopify.com/blogs/news/7406100-getting-started-video` in order to understand how to put the sensor correctly on your finger.

You can now upload the code to your Arduino board and open the serial monitor. Then place the sensor on your finger. After a while (there can be strange readings at first), you should see your heart rate being displayed on the serial monitor. You will know that it is correct when the value is between 60 and 100 BPM (if you are in a resting state).

Writing the Arduino sketch

Now that we are sure that the sensor is working correctly, we can write the final Arduino sketch for this chapter. This sketch will perform the BPM measurements as before, and will also expose the BPM variable via the aREST API so that the measurements can be accessed via Bluetooth. As the sketch is really similar to the test sketch, we will only detail the changes here.

The sketch starts by importing the required libraries:

```
#include <SPI.h>
#include "Adafruit_BLE_UART.h"
#include <aREST.h>
```

We also define the pins on which the BLE module is connected:

```
#define ADAFRUITBLE_REQ 10
#define ADAFRUITBLE_RDY 2     // This should be an interrupt pin, on
Uno thats #2 or #3
#define ADAFRUITBLE_RST 9
```

Then we create an instance of the aREST library and the BLE module:

```
aREST rest = aREST();

// BLE instance
Adafruit_BLE_UART BTLEserial = Adafruit_BLE_UART(ADAFRUITBLE_REQ,
ADAFRUITBLE_RDY, ADAFRUITBLE_RST);
```

We also need to define a variable that will contain the BPM measurements and that will be exposed to the API:

```
int bpm = 0;
```

In the `setup()` function, we need to initialize the BLE module:

```
BTLEserial.begin();
```

We also give the project a name and ID:

```
rest.set_id("1");
rest.set_name("pulse_sensor");
```

Still in the `setup()` function, we expose the BPM variable to the aREST API:

```
rest.variable("bpm",&bpm);
```

In the `loop()` function of the sketch, we assign the measured BPM to the variable that is exposed to the API:

```
bpm = BPM;
```

Then, as usual, we process the incoming requests on the BLE module with the aREST API:

```
// Tell the nRF8001 to do whatever it should be working on.
BTLEserial.pollACI();

// Ask what is our current status
aci_evt_opcode_t status = BTLEserial.getState();

// Handle REST calls
if (status == ACI_EVT_CONNECTED) {
    rest.handle(BTLEserial);
  }
}
```

Note that all the code for this chapter can be found in the GitHub repository of the bookat `https://github.com/marcoschwartz/arduino-android-blueprints`. You can now upload the code to your Arduino board and move on to the development of the Android application.

Setting up the Android app

The Android application that we will be creating will give us the ability to display the data that is measured by the pulse rate sensor within the Android app. In addition, it will show the BLE connection status, and there will be the **Refresh** button to allow us to refresh the Bluetooth callback.

We will assume that you will have switched on the `Auto-Import` function within your preferences. If not, kindly activate it by going to the **Auto-Import** preferences and selecting all available options. The **Auto-Import** preferences are available on Mac and Windows as follows:

- On a Mac, navigate to **Android Studio** > **Preferences** > **Editor** > **Auto-Import**
- On Windows, navigate to **File** > **Settings** > **Editor** > **Auto-Import**

With all the necessary settings in place, we will start off by creating a new project where we will choose the following within the **New Project** setup walkthrough:

- **Name**: `Pulse Rate Sensor`
- **Minimum SDK**: `18`
- **Project**: `Blank Activity`
- **Activity Name**: `PulseActivity`
- **Domain**: `arduinoandroid.com`

Laying out the Android user interface and setting permissions

In order to make this project work, we will need to first go to the Android `Manifest` file which is available at `app` > `src` > `main` > `AndroidManifest.xml`.

Since this Android application uses BLE to connect the Android physical device to the pulse rate sensor, we will need to add the following permissions to the Android `Manifest` file:

```
    <uses-permission android:name="android.permission.BLUETOOTH"/>
    <uses-permission android:name="android.permission.BLUETOOTH_
ADMIN"/>
```

The next step that we will be taking is setting up the very basic Android layout file so that we are able to implement the app functions.

In our project, we will navigate to the main layout file which can be accessed from `app` > `src` > `res` > `layout` > `activity_pulse.xml`.

There are a number of layout formats with Android user interface design, and in this particular case, we will be implementing two linear layouts: one will be designed to act as a placeholder for the graph view, and the other will support the different buttons and text views.

Replace the current code available in the layout file with the following code:

```
<?xml version="1.0" encoding="utf-8"?>

<LinearLayout
    xmlns:android="http://schemas.android.com/apk/res/android"
    android:orientation="vertical"
    android:layout_width="fill_parent"
    android:layout_height="fill_parent">

    <LinearLayout
        android:id="@+id/rest"
        android:layout_width="fill_parent"
        android:layout_height="250dip"
        android:orientation="vertical"
        android:weightSum="1">

        <TextView
            android:layout_width="match_parent"
            android:layout_height="wrap_content"
            android:textAppearance="?android:attr/textAppearanceLarge"
            android:id="@+id/pulseValueView"
            android:layout_gravity="center_horizontal"
            android:textSize="150dp"
            android:gravity="center"
            android:text="120"/>
    </LinearLayout>

    <Button
        android:layout_width="wrap_content"
        android:layout_height="wrap_content"
        android:text="Refresh Connection"
        android:id="@+id/refreshBtn"
        android:layout_gravity="center_horizontal" />
```

```
        <Button
            android:layout_width="wrap_content"
            android:layout_height="wrap_content"
            android:text="Get Pulse Rate"
            android:id="@+id/heartRateBtn"
            android:layout_gravity="center_horizontal" />

        <TextView
            android:layout_width="wrap_content"
            android:layout_height="wrap_content"
            android:textAppearance="?android:attr/textAppearanceLarge"
            android:text="Connection Status"
            android:id="@+id/connectionStsView"
            android:layout_gravity="center_horizontal" />
    </LinearLayout>
```

The end result will look as follows within the IDE:

The text **120** is meant to be a placeholder text to ensure that there is enough place within the user interface to accommodate the pulse rate readings. In the final implementation, you have the option of removing the placeholder text and leaving it blank.

Coding the app's internals

We need to start off by declaring all the necessary variables that are needed to work with the Bluetooth logic, user interface, and for logging purposes:

```
    //Logging Variables
    private final String LOG_TAG = PulseActivity.class.
getSimpleName();

    //User Interface Variables
    Button getPulseRate;
    Button refreshButton;
    TextView pulseRateView;
    TextView connectionStsView;

    //Data Output
    private String output;

    // UUIDs for UAT service and associated characteristics.
    public static UUID UART_UUID = UUID.fromString("6E400001-B5A3-
F393-E0A9-E50E24DCCA9E");
    public static UUID TX_UUID = UUID.fromString("6E400002-B5A3-F393-
E0A9-E50E24DCCA9E");
    public static UUID RX_UUID = UUID.fromString("6E400003-B5A3-F393-
E0A9-E50E24DCCA9E");

    // UUID for the BTLE client characteristic which is necessary for
notifications.
    public static UUID CLIENT_UUID = UUID.fromString("00002902-0000-
1000-8000-00805f9b34fb");

    // BTLE stateta
    private BluetoothAdapter adapter;
    private BluetoothGatt gatt;
    private BluetoothGattCharacteristic tx;
    private BluetoothGattCharacteristic rx;

    private boolean areServicesAccessible = false;
```

Following this, we will need to connect the user interface elements within the `onCreate()` method to the user interface, and set an `onClickListener` class to the **Get Pulse Rate** and **Refresh** buttons, which will allow us to request the pulse rate sensor data and refresh Bluetooth connections:

```
        //Connect U.I Elements
        getPulseRate = (Button) findViewById(R.id.heartRateBtn);
        pulseRateView = (TextView) findViewById(R.id.pulseValueView);
        connectionStsView = (TextView) findViewById(R.
id.connectionStsView);
        refreshButton = (Button) findViewById(R.id.refreshBtn);


        getPulseRate.setOnClickListener(new View.OnClickListener() {
            @Override
            public void onClick(View view) {
                String setOutputMessage = "/bpm /";
                tx.setValue(setOutputMessage.getBytes(Charset.
forName("UTF-8")));
                if (gatt.writeCharacteristic(tx)) {
                    writeConnectionData("Sent: " + setOutputMessage);
                } else {
                    writeConnectionData("Couldn't write TX
characteristic!");
                }
            }
        });

        refreshButton.setOnClickListener(new View.OnClickListener() {
            @Override
            public void onClick(View view) {
                restartScan();
            }
        });
    }
```

Since we are using Bluetooth in our projects, we need to implement the methods that allow us to take the character data sequences, convert them into string, and finally connect them to the user interface to display the data:

```
    private void writeConnectionData(final CharSequence text) {
        Log.e(LOG_TAG, text.toString());
```

```
        connectionStsView.setText(text.toString());
    }

    private void writeSensorData(final CharSequence text) {
        runOnUiThread(new Runnable() {
            @Override
            public void run() {
                Log.e(LOG_TAG,text.toString());
                output=text.toString().trim();

                if (output.length() > 0 && output.length() <=3) {
                    pulseRateView.setText(output);
                }
                else {
                    return;
                }
            }
        });
    }
```

The following methods will allow us to do the necessary Bluetooth callback and send or receive data from the Arduino pulse rate sensor via the BLE module:

```
    // BTLE device scanning bluetoothGattCallback.

    // Main BTLE device bluetoothGattCallback where much of the logic
occurs.
    private BluetoothGattCallback bluetoothGattCallback = new
BluetoothGattCallback() {
        // Called whenever the device connection state changes, i.e.
from disconnected to connected.
        @Override
        public void onConnectionStateChange(BluetoothGatt gatt, int
status, int newState) {
            super.onConnectionStateChange(gatt, status, newState);
            if (newState == BluetoothGatt.STATE_CONNECTED) {
                writeConnectionData("Connected!");
                // Discover services.
                if (!gatt.discoverServices()) {
                    writeConnectionData("Failed to start discovering
services!");
                }
```

```
            } else if (newState == BluetoothGatt.STATE_DISCONNECTED) {
                writeConnectionData("Disconnected!");
            } else {
                writeConnectionData("Connection state changed.  New
state: " + newState);
            }
        }

        // Called when services have been discovered on the remote
device.
        // It seems to be necessary to wait for this discovery to
occur before
        // manipulating any services or characteristics.
        public void onServicesDiscovered(BluetoothGatt gatt, int
status) {
            super.onServicesDiscovered(gatt, status);
            if (status == BluetoothGatt.GATT_SUCCESS) {
                writeConnectionData("Service discovery completed!");
            } else {
                writeConnectionData("Service discovery failed with
status: " + status);
            }
            // Save reference to each characteristic.
            tx = gatt.getService(UART_UUID).getCharacteristic(TX_
UUID);
            rx = gatt.getService(UART_UUID).getCharacteristic(RX_
UUID);

            // Setup notifications on RX characteristic changes (i.e.
data received).
            // First call setCharacteristicNotification to enable
notification.
            if (!gatt.setCharacteristicNotification(rx, true)) {
                writeConnectionData("Couldn't set notifications for RX
characteristic!");
            }

            // Next update the RX characteristic's client descriptor
to enable notifications.
            if (rx.getDescriptor(CLIENT_UUID) != null) {
                BluetoothGattDescriptor desc =
rx.getDescriptor(CLIENT_UUID);
                desc.setValue(BluetoothGattDescriptor.ENABLE_
NOTIFICATION_VALUE);
```

```
                if (!gatt.writeDescriptor(desc)) {
                    writeConnectionData("Couldn't write RX client
descriptor value!");
                }
            } else {
                writeConnectionData("Couldn't get RX client
descriptor!");
            }
            areServicesAccessible = true;
        }
        // Called when a remote characteristic changes (like the RX
characteristic).
        @Override
        public void onCharacteristicChanged(BluetoothGatt gatt,
BluetoothGattCharacteristic characteristic) {
            super.onCharacteristicChanged(gatt, characteristic);
            writeSensorData(characteristic.getStringValue(0));
        }
    };


private BluetoothAdapter.LeScanCallback scanCallback = new
BluetoothAdapter.LeScanCallback() {
        // Called when a device is found.
        @Override
        public void onLeScan(BluetoothDevice bluetoothDevice, int i,
byte[] bytes) {
            Log.d(LOG_TAG, bluetoothDevice.getAddress());

            writeConnectionData("Found device: " + bluetoothDevice.
getAddress());

            // Check if the device has the UART service.
            if (BluetoothUtils.parseUUIDs(bytes).contains(UART_UUID))
{
                // Found a device, stop the scan.
                adapter.stopLeScan(scanCallback);
                writeConnectionData("Found UART service!");
                // Connect to the device.
                // Control flow will now go to the
bluetoothGattCallback functions when BTLE events occur.
                gatt = bluetoothDevice.connectGatt(getApplicationConte
xt(), false, bluetoothGattCallback);
            }
        }
    };
}
```

The Android application life cycle allows us to implement methods at its different stages, so in the following code, we will be implementing two methods which allow us to start Bluetooth scanning when the application is activated, and stop Bluetooth scanning and other related activities when the user exits the application:

```
    protected void onStart() {
        Log.d(LOG_TAG,"onStart has been called");
        super.onStart();
        // / Scan for all BTLE devices.
        // The first one with the UART service will be chosen--see the
code in the scanCallback.
        adapter = BluetoothAdapter.getDefaultAdapter();
        startScan();
    }

    //When this Activity isn't visible anymore
    protected void onStop() {
        Log.d(LOG_TAG,"onStop has been called");
        //disconnect and close Bluetooth Connection for better
reliability
        if (gatt != null) {
            gatt.disconnect();
            gatt.close();
            gatt = null;
            tx = null;
            rx = null;
        }
        super.onStop();
    }
```

We will also be including a number of methods that facilitate the BLE scan callback and enable us to refactor the code and keep our code clean:

```
    //BLUETOOTH METHODS
    private void startScan() {
        if (!adapter.isEnabled()) {
            adapter.enable();
        }
        if (!adapter.isDiscovering()) {
            adapter.startDiscovery();
        }
        writeConnectionData("Scanning for devices...");
        adapter.startLeScan(scanCallback);
    }
```

```
    private void stopScan() {
        if (adapter.isDiscovering()) {
            adapter.cancelDiscovery();
        }
        writeConnectionData("Stopping scan");
        adapter.stopLeScan(scanCallback);
    }

    private void restartScan() {
        stopScan();
        startScan();
    }
```

UUID parsing, unlike the previous chapters, has been moved to a `utility` class in order to refactor the code and make it more readable. In order to create a `utility` class, we first need to right-click on our package name and create a new package called `Bluetooth`.

Then we will right-click on the new package, select **New** > **Java Class**, and name the new class as `BluetoothUtils`.

After these two steps, we will replace the code within the class with the following code:

```
public class BluetoothUtils {

    // Filtering by custom UUID is broken in Android 4.3 and 4.4, see:
    //   http://stackoverflow.com/questions/18019161/startlescan-with-
128-bit-uuids-doesnt-work-on-native-android-ble-implementation?noredir
ect=1#comment27879874_18019161
    // This is a workaround function from the SO thread to manually
parse advertisement data.
    public static List<UUID> parseUUIDs(final byte[] advertisedData) {
        List<UUID> uuids = new ArrayList<UUID>();

        int offset = 0;
        while (offset < (advertisedData.length - 2)) {
            int len = advertisedData[offset++];
            if (len == 0)
                break;

            int type = advertisedData[offset++];
            switch (type) {
                case 0x02: // Partial list of 16-bit UUIDs
                case 0x03: // Complete list of 16-bit UUIDs
                    while (len > 1) {
                        int uuid16 = advertisedData[offset++];
```

```
                        uuid16 += (advertisedData[offset++] << 8);
                        len -= 2;
                        uuids.add(UUID.fromString(String.format("%08x-
0000-1000-8000-00805f9b34fb", uuid16)));
                    }
                    break;
                case 0x06:// Partial list of 128-bit UUIDs
                case 0x07:// Complete list of 128-bit UUIDs
                    // Loop through the advertised 128-bit UUID's.
                    while (len >= 16) {
                        try {
                            // Wrap the advertised bits and order
them.
                            ByteBuffer buffer = ByteBuffer.
wrap(advertisedData, offset++, 16).order(ByteOrder.LITTLE_ENDIAN);
                            long mostSignificantBit = buffer.
getLong();
                            long leastSignificantBit = buffer.
getLong();
                            uuids.add(new UUID(leastSignificantBit,
                                    mostSignificantBit));
                        } catch (IndexOutOfBoundsException e) {
                            // Defensive programming.
                            //Log.e(LOG_TAG, e.toString());
                            continue;
                        } finally {
                            // Move the offset to read the next uuid.
                            offset += 15;
                            len -= 16;
                        }
                    }
                    break;
                default:
                    offset += (len - 1);
                    break;
            }
        }
        return uuids;
    }
}
```

At this point, you could go ahead, build, and run the project on an Android physical device running on Android 4.3 with Bluetooth switched on. In order to get your pulse rate in this project, you will need to follow the instructions as mentioned previously and tap on the **Get Pulse Rate** button.

How to go further

We believe that this project can be taken further by possibly including other health-related sensors that are available from a number of online outlets and displaying the related data within a graph.

The Android graph view library supports multiple inputs using multiple series. Further information about this can be obtained at the official website for documentation at `http://android-graphview.org/`.

A screenshot of how this application could possibly look with Android graph view would be similar to the following:

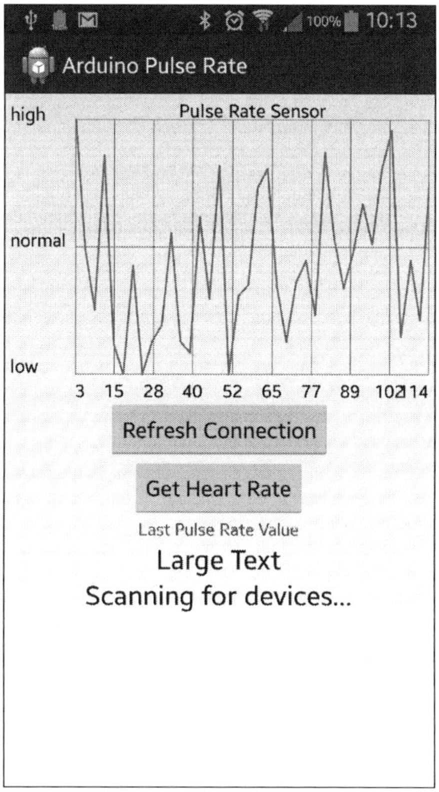

Further improvements could also be done to the user interface and user experience where the data can be updated in real time via handler or timer implementations. Finally, one of the most advanced integrations that could be included in this kind of application is integration with the Google Fit SDK, which is Google's proprietary health data platform. Another option could be storage of health data using cloud storage APIs and local databases.

Summary

In this chapter, we integrated what we had learned from the previous chapters and created a baseline project to measure our own pulse rate.

We achieved this by creating an Android app which shows the data produced by the pulse rate sensor connected to the Arduino Uno. Communication between both devices is via BLE.

The baseline projects that we have introduced throughout this book are present to motivate you to be creative and solve your daily challenges. We have realized that the possibilities of combining Arduino and Android are endless, and we hope that you will stretch the limitations of what is possible.

Index

Symbols

A

B

C

D

F

G

H

I

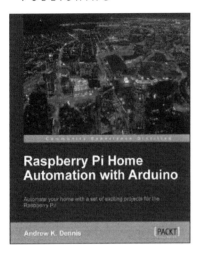

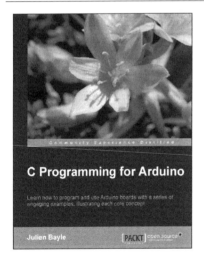

[PACKT] open source
community experience distilled
PUBLISHING

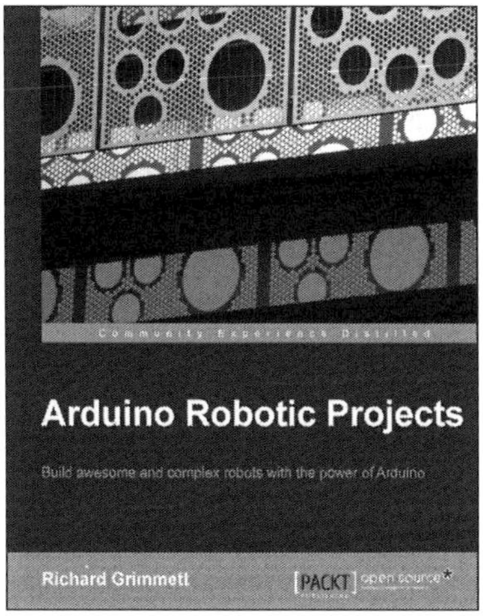

Arduino Robotic Projects

ISBN: 978-1-78398-982-9 Paperback: 240 pages

Build awesome and complex robots with the power of Arduino

1. Develop a series of exciting robots that can sail, go under water, and fly.
2. Simple, easy-to-understand instructions to program Arduino.
3. Effectively control the movements of all types of motors using Arduino.

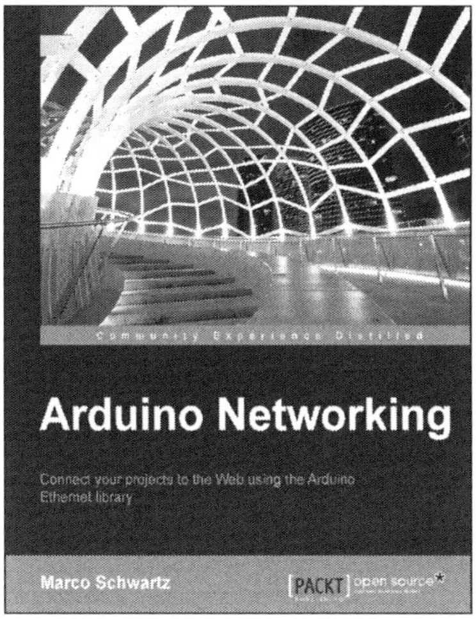

Arduino Networking

ISBN: 978-1-78398-686-6 Paperback: 118 pages

Connect your projects to the Web using the Arduino Ethernet library

1. Learn to use the Arduino Ethernet shield and Ethernet library.
2. Control the Arduino projects from your computer using the Arduino Ethernet.
3. This is a step-by-step guide to creating Internet of Things projects using the Arduino Ethernet shield.

Please check **www.PacktPub.com** for information on our titles

9177803R00139

Printed in Great Britain
by Amazon.co.uk, Ltd.,
Marston Gate.